# GOD'S BEST TO YOU

I appreciate knowing
you. You are wonderful
Christians.
Jerry Haynes

# GOD'S BEST TO YOU

Jerry Hayner

BROADMAN PRESS
Nashville, Tennessee

4251-92
ISBN: 0-8054-5192-7
Dewey Decimal Classification: 242
Subject Heading: MEDITATIONS

Library of Congress Catalog Card Number: 81-71257
Printed in the United States of America

To Karen, Kelli, and Todd—
three of God's very best
gifts he has allowed me
to enjoy.

# Preface

"How can anyone have faith and hope in a world like this?" That's the question one man asked his minister. It's not an unusual question. A lot of people have the thought even if they never express it openly. Most of us are far more familiar with despair and helplessness than we would like to be. Day by day, we live in the midst of some seemingly hopeless situations. Faith and hope are luxuries that some people feel they can't afford.

But the good news of Jesus Christ is just that—good news. Read his story. Listen to his words. Observe how he related to people. Through it all you'll be captured by the fact that Jesus really believed. His faith in God was not that of a timid soul reaching out through a fantasy toward the future. His hope was not the simple "I hope so" that characterizes our speech. Jesus identified God as giving him "all power in heaven and in earth." He asked his disciples to go in that power, and "lo, I am with you alway" (Matt. 28:18-20). Just to read the final chapter of Matthew's Gospel gives one the feeling of conquest.

Yet many of us who call ourselves "Christians" are not living as conquerors. Why? Is it because the Christian gospel is a myth, a fairy tale, the vain babblings of a deluded first-century dreamer? Or is it because we are not claiming the power, the authority, the Presence of the living Christ?

The first book I wrote was called *Say Hello to Life*. My aim was to challenge people to find the abundant life about which Jesus spoke in John 10. This book is a follow-up on that theme. Abundant life, victorious life, life with a capital L—that's what I want. I think that's what most people want. Why don't we experience it? I'm convinced that just as God wants us to have that kind of life, the power of evil is at work in the world preventing us from enjoying it.

This book is built around some important words—*life, free, help, care, love,* and *hope*. Jesus frequently used these words. A right understanding of these words can help lead us to that abundant life, that victorious, fulfilled life we seek.

*God's Best to You* is a positive approach to living. Some negative ways of thinking will be challenged in this book. I don't know where you are in your life right now, but I'm confident that God has some good news for you. Maybe some of that good news will be presented in the chapters you're about to read.

I've chosen to include ten messages under each of the six themes. These messages are accompanied by Scripture verses that are pertinent. They also contain thoughts from other writers about the same subject discussed. Each will then close with a brief prayer.

You may choose to use these as daily devotionals. You may choose to use them as conversation starters in a Bible study group. However the Spirit of God uses these thoughts, it is my prayer that you will be strengthened and encouraged. I truly want GOD'S BEST to be given TO YOU.

# Contents

# GOD'S BEST TO YOU

# 1
# LIFE

What a beautiful word that is! When one thinks about life, all kinds of thoughts surge to the top of one's mind. Good thoughts. Bad thoughts. Pleasant memories. Sad memories. The past. The present. The future. Ourselves. Others. Perhaps we think of where we are in life right now, our successes, our failures, our hopes, our dreams. Jesus said, "I am the way, the truth, and the life" (John 14:16). Life really finds its deepest meaning in Christ, in the reality that it is he who gives life. John said, "But these have been written that you may believe that Jesus is the Christ, the Son of God; and that believing you may have life in His name" (John 20:31, NASB). God's best to you is life . . . abundant life . . . eternal life.

## When the Heart Is Hungry

Someone asked, "What does it take to make a person happy?" And someone answered, "Just a little bit more." Unfortunately, we human beings seem to be made that way. Our desires remain limitless. We get some things. We want some more. We earn some money. We want more.

Part of the problem is within our imagination. We have the ability to imagine what life would be like "if" . . . if I had more money . . . if I had a better situation . . . if I had more of this or that. As soon as some desire has seen its goal accomplished, our imaginations take over and create a desire for more.

Is that bad? In some ways, it isn't. That's why we accomplish some of the things we might not achieve otherwise. I'm glad that people were not satisfied with the discovery of the wheel. We've improved upon that discovery, and we'll improve some more. I'm glad we had ancestors who were not satisfied with the mere occupation of the new land. They wanted more than quantity. They wanted quality, and throughout history, we have been trying to make the good into something better.

What I am concerned about is the lack of fulfillment so many of us have in the midst of all of this. Far too many people are living restless, unfulfilled, meaningless existences. Far too many are saying:

> . . . it [life] is a tale
> Told by an idiot, full of sound and fury,
> Signifying nothing.[1]

Leonard Griffith told about a visit he made to the home of a very wealthy man. The man lived in a house that was richly furnished. It was equipped with five bathrooms. Expensive mirrors lined the walls. Ornate decorations were spread throughout the house. In the library there were more books than he could possibly read. There was also a bar laden with the finest of wines and liquors. He had sports equipment in abundance, and on one shelf were three electric razors.

"You have so much," Griffith remarked. "Yes," the man sadly replied, "but the trouble with having a lot of things is that you don't control them; they control you." And so many times, they do.

Jesus said something very profound at this point. "'A man's life does not consist in the abundance of his possessions'" (Luke 12:15, RSV). A person does not satisfy an internal hunger by external decorations or amusements. Many people who have so much are enjoying it so little. Why? Because God has said there is more to life than the pleasures and toys the world has to offer.

You and I are spiritual beings. When the heart is hungry, a gold bracelet or a fancy sports car will not meet its need. Only God can satisfy our deepest hunger. Isn't it time we learned that? Isn't it time we turned around and sat at his table?

**The Lord says,**
**"Come, everyone who is thirsty—**
**here is water!**
**Come, you that have no money—**
**buy grain and eat!**
**Come! Buy wine and milk—**
**it will cost you nothing!**
**Why spend money on what does not satisfy?**
**Why spend your wages and still be hungry?**
**Listen to me and do what I say,**
**and you will enjoy the best food of all."**
**(Isa. 55:1-2, TEV)**

In every one of us there is no stronger drive than the desire for happiness. It is so strong that as soon as we achieve one happy goal we are immediately on the lookout for new shapes and forms of happiness. . . . So happiness is constantly changing its shape and is always just ahead of us. For one it may be money and success, for another the satisfaction of accomplishment, for another the comfort and peace of being at home at one's own hearth. But whatever form it may take, we all pursue it.[2]

*Lord, within my heart there is a deep restlessness, a longing for something more, something better. Is that my earthly desire for heaven, not hereafter but here and now? Have you made us all that way? If so, help me not to try to feed my heavenly desires with earthly things. Today, let me sit at your table. In Jesus' name, I pray. Amen.*

## A Two-Feather Tail

The good doctor, a man named Seuss, told the story about a jealous bird named Gertrude McFuzz.[3] It seemed that our Miss, Mrs., or Ms. McFuzz had only one droopy feather for a tail, and the quite attractive Lolla-Lee-Lou had a "two-feather tail." Of course, everyone knows that a two-feather tail is more attractive than a one-feather tail, so something had to be done about that.

Poor Gertrude was just eaten up with envy. More than one time she dropped a worm out of her mouth when pretty Lolla-Lee-Lou passed by. She kicked a few sticks here and there until her pointed toes were blue with bruises. She fussed to her family and friends until no one wanted to have her around.

Finally, when she could take it no longer, she went to see her doctor. He in turn directed her to a pill-berry vine, where, when she ate a pill berry, a new tail feather would appear. I suppose that would be comparable to having a face-lifting, a new car with an AM-FM stereo with tape deck and quadraphonic speakers, or maybe even a new body without spot, wrinkle, or shimmy. Anyway, dear Gertrude was at the top of her game. She had received a prescription for beauty, a chance to "keep up with the Joneses," a new lease on life.

She couldn't run fast enough to get to the pill-berry vine.

Furthermore, after having gotten there, she used poor judgment in trying to satisfy her greed. One pill berry would give one new tail feather. Two pill berries would give two. Aiming to be prettier than NBC's peacock, Gertrude took a mouthful of the pill berries, and she received a tail full of brilliant feathers. Her only problem was that now she couldn't fly. She was so determined to be the prettiest bird on the block that she forgot what it really meant to be a bird, to be able to fly. She had won her battle with Lolla-Lee-Lou, but the poor girl had lost the war.

That story wouldn't be so sad if it weren't so true of a few of us "birds." Discontented with our own situations, we are always in search of a few more "tail feathers." We have a desire to want to be the best in everything. We have a fear of being overlooked or left out. And most of us have those emotions that make us jealous or covetous of the situations or belongings of others.

Happy is the person who can accept his own uniqueness, who does not spend his time comparing himself to what others look like or have, who can approvingly say, "I am God's gift to me."

The people who are really "flying" are the ones who have settled the tail-feather issue. They have submitted themselves to God and are serving in his name. Believe me—that's where the real joy is!

**"When my thoughts were bitter**
**and my feelings were hurt,**
**I was as stupid as an animal;**
**I did not understand you.**

**. . . . . . . . . . . . . . . . . . . . . . . . . . . . . . . . . . . . . . . .**

**What else do I have in heaven but you?**
**Since I have you, what else could I want on earth?"**
**(Ps. 73:21-22,25, TEV)**

If you can "see" yourself as potentially a highly effective personality, able to give and receive love, and to achieve far more than you have up to this time—if you set this goal-seeking mechanism to work, all of your inner forces, and the power of God working in you, are available to bring it into reality.[4]

*Lord, I suppose we're all somewhat like poor Gertrude. We tend to compare ourselves with others, and more often than not, we concentrate on those things and attributes which they have that we don't. I don't know why we can't see that we might have some gifts they don't have. Anyway, help me to just try to be the best that I can be with the gifts you have given me. Then perhaps I will have inner peace. Amen.*

## "Pints, Quarts, and All That Stuff"

"A teaspoonful of this, a dash of that, stir in together and mix in with a half-pint of milk"—and so the recipe goes, on and on. The temperature comes by Fahrenheit and Celsius, the miles are registered by kilometers, and the slide rule is used for a hundred different things.

We live by measurements. In almost everything we do we are confronted with size, distance, temperature, and other such means which we have developed for keeping things in order.

I know that we measure distance by inches, feet, yards, and miles. I know that we measure electrical power by kilowatts and voltage. I know there are ounces, pints, quarts, and gallons for the measurement of our liquid products.

But how do you measure a life? Some people measure it by its accumulation. "He's worth a lot of money," they say. Some people measure it by its influence. "She's a great woman. People know her name from coast to coast."

How do you measure a life? Some say that you measure it by months and years, and some say it is to be measured by its smiles and tears. But how do you measure the worth of a life? Can you take away one of twelve children from the mother and comfort her by saying, "Don't be upset! You've got eleven left"? Will she grieve any less because she has lost only one?

How can you measure what a person is worth to life? Some say that life can be measured by its duration. If that is true, then some small men are great because they live a long time, and some great men are small because they die prematurely. The Bible and history are filled with the names of men and women who lived long lives, but who made little, if any, lasting contribution that is worthwhile.

How do you measure the value of a life? If not by its duration, then perhaps by its donation—what it gives, what it deposits, what it leaves for others. Yes, perhaps that's it—its donation, its contribution. Maybe that's the way you measure a life. I think it is.

Some of the best books I have read have not been the longest ones. The author was able to say what he wanted to say in a few pages, and he left me hungering for more. But more importantly, he left a profound influence on my thinking. Some of the best music I have heard has not been the seemingly endless oratorios or symphonies—no, just a few lines, a few bars, a few notes—but they were filled with meaning and melody.

No one knows how long he will live. That's not altogether ours to choose, unless we choose to limit our life by taking it. We cannot choose the quantity of time that we shall have, but we can have something to say about the quality. We cannot choose the length of life, but we can choose the depth.

Christ said it this way: "For whoever wants to save his own life will lose it; but whoever loses his life for my sake will find it" (Matt. 16:25, TEV). Give your life to God. Give it for the good of others. It'll be worth more in the long run.

**An argument broke out among the disciples as to which one of them should be thought of as the greatest. Jesus said to them, "The kings of the pagans have power over their people, and the rulers are called 'Friends of the People.' But this is not the way it is with you; rather, the greatest one among you must be like the youngest, and the leader must be like the servant." (Luke 22:24-26, TEV)**

> "He that would lose his life for my sake shall find it." This glorious truth is the wisdom of all ages compressed into one blessed sentence. Since God's prescription for genuine living revolves around the verb "to give" instead of "to get," then to give oneself is a happy, though sometimes painful experience. Self-giving is our desperate need![5]

*Lord, in a world where we are so conscious about who we are and what we have, when we spend so much time comparing ourselves with others, help us to learn the art of self-forgetfulness so that we can get on with making some contribution to life. I ask but one thing, Lord. May the world be a better place when I leave it because I have been here. Amen.*

## Signs of Our Times

You've seen the signs. They're everywhere. "Slow Down and Live." "The Hurrieder I Go, The Behinder I Get." R. A. Lafferty said it this way, "And then the world came to an end, only everyone was too busy to notice, so they went right on doing what they always did."

Signs of our times are everywhere—nervous breakdowns, mental collapses, heart attacks. These signs ought to tell us something about the rate of speed with which we're driving ourselves. Another sign said: "Death is nature's way of saying 'Slow Down.'" Signs of our times!

Most people are plagued by their "have to's," "oughts," "shoulds," "musts," and "what will people think if I don'ts?" It seems we're constantly being urged by some kind of compulsion, either external or internal. Little we see in nature that gets our attention. Little we see in others that we can pause to appreciate. Little we see in life that we can truly enjoy.

The pace is fast. We drive fast, eat fast, walk fast, and die fast. Oh, I know, we are living longer than any generation of Americans in history. Let's put it this way—we're physically alive. But many people are not enjoying life. Perhaps most people are not experiencing life in all its fullness. How can we? The projector is putting the pictures on the screen and taking them off faster than we can focus on them. Such is life for many of us. The signs of our times!

Why the hurry? Maybe we're afraid we're going to miss something. We've got to rush from place to place, person to person, experience to experience to make certain that something that might be exciting will not be missed. We don't like second-hand information. We want to experience it all for ourselves. So . . . "I'll talk to you later. I have to go now. There are too many things to do."

Perhaps it's because others have forced us onto this treadmill. "You've just got to come to my party. I'll be so disappointed if you don't." "Please try to attend all of the meetings." How does one respond to the pressure? We're so afraid of offending others that we push, push, push.

Jesus intrigues me. He seemed never to be in a hurry even when people tried to "push" him. A man's daughter was dying, but Jesus stopped to heal a woman who for twelve years had been unable to find health. People in the city were waiting to hear him teach, but he stopped and blessed the children. He was on his way to Jerusalem when he heard the pathetic cries of a beggar and stopped to help him. The story he told about the good Samaritan was the story of men in a hurry who would not stop, and a "good" Samaritan who did.

The pace is killing us. That's for certain. Life is passing us by, and we're the losers. Most of us would do well to pray, "Slow me down, Lord,/Ease the pounding of my heart by the quieting of my mind" (Samuel Miller Hageman).

"Be still, and know that I am God" saith the Lord (Ps. 46:10). Who has time to "be still"? "Excuse me, I've got to go. I'm already late for an appointment." That's a sign of something. "Speed Kills." It's just a matter of time.

**Now listen to me, you that say, "Today or tomorrow we will travel to a certain city, where we will stay a year and go into business and make a lot of money." You don't even know what your life tomorrow will be! You are like a puff of smoke, which appears for a moment and then disappears. (Jas. 4:13-14, TEV)**

> A compulsive person tends to be formal, meticulous, perfectionistic, overly inhibited, self-doubting, and fastidious. He is often compelled by forces from within that he does not understand to perform activities which he would rather not

> undertake. . . . This person with compulsive tendencies finds it hard to relax, follows a literal obedience, has an exaggerated sensitivity, often is stubborn, and feels harassed by responsibility.[6]

*Lord, somewhere in your word I read that you "rested." How did you find time to do that? I also read somewhere that your Son asked us to come to him, and he would give us rest.*

*Father in heaven, help me to know that if you found it possible and practical to rest, so can I. Through Jesus Christ, I pray. Amen.*

## "The Saddest Are These"

The story has been told about an elderly man who brought some sketches he had made to Dante G. Rossetti, the poet and painter. Rossetti examined them carefully and then told the man they had no value. The old man then placed before the artist some sketches made by a student. Rossetti looked at them and enthusiastically told the man to encourage that student. The old gentleman was moved to tears. He said, "Sir, I was that student!"

I wonder how many times a story like that could be repeated with different characters and different issues. Life is literally filled with people who began well but finished poorly. Some people have had great gifts to give, but they never gave them. They have had magnificent talents, but they never used them.

Everyone is gifted. As infants we come into this world with great potential. Unfortunately, due to some strong influences and due to some unfavorable environmental situations, some of us never are able to realize the fullness of that potential. How many promising artists, writers, or doctors have had to shift gears and go in another direction in order to supply some pressing family need? About how many people has it been said at some time early in their lives, "He will go far"? Yet, not too many people go far. Some rise a little above their peers, but most slip back into mediocrity, never achieving their vast potential. Why?

For some, it was a question of "too much too soon." The

applause they received early caused them to mistake their progress at that point with the destination. "I'm good enough," some have said to themselves, "why try any harder? Let the world catch up with me." And indeed, the "world" did catch up and passed them.

For some, it has been a matter of poor leadership. Parents are at fault many times. When their sons or daughters have asked for bread, something that would help them grow and develop, they have given them a stone. Sometimes those stones have come in the form of monuments—"Son, daughter, you're the greatest!" And the son or daughter failed to strive for more. Sometimes those stones have been in the form of rocks—rocks thrown at the child, discouragement, put-downs, unjust criticism, nagging.

As John Greenleaf Whittier wrote, "Of all sad words of tongue or pen,/the saddest are these: 'It might have been!'" And so it is. More could be written about what "might have been" than about "what is."

Jesus once said to his disciples, "Follow me, and I will make you become . . . " (Mark 1:17, RSV). And throughout their lives that process of becoming continued. I hope you are still in the process of becoming all that God meant for you to be. Paul said, "I do not claim that I have already succeeded or have already become perfect. I keep striving to win the prize for which Christ Jesus has already won me to himself" (Phil. 4:12, TEV). If he could say that, how much more should we try to reach our fullest potential for God?

**To him who by means of his power working in us is able to do so much more than we can ever ask for, or even think of: to God be the glory in the church and in Christ Jesus for all time, forever and ever! Amen. (Eph. 3:20-21, TEV)**

> All life is an adventure, and all adventure has its difficulties. The path of life is always strewn with failures. What complicates the problem still further is that life's successes are as dangerous as its failures. "I fear success more than anything," wrote Bernard Shaw. "To have succeeded means that one has

> finished one's work on this earth. . . . Life has meaning for me only if it remains a perpetual beginning, a definite goal in front of one and not behind." This is the paradoxical law of adventure, namely, that the thing that puts an end to it is its success. Success is perilous.[7]

*With so much that needs to be done in our world, and with so little time in which to do it, help me, O God, not to be satisfied to quit. Keep me hungry for the adventure. Like Paul, help me to keep running the race until you say, "That's enough." In Jesus' name I pray, Amen.*

## Running Away

Have you ever wanted to run away . . . I mean, far, far away? Perhaps it doesn't matter where you might arrive. Just to get away from it all—that is what matters.

Running, jogging, or whatever you want to call it, is in great vogue everywhere. It isn't unusual at all to see people jogging very early in the morning or late at night. But as popular as that means of recreation might be, it isn't as common as "running away." And one thing about "running away" is that you can do that without ever leaving your spot, without lifting a finger, without exercising a muscle, except maybe the "muscles" of your mind.

Running away is as popular as daydreaming, as common as wishing, as current as this moment. Maybe it's a condition that affects all of us at one time or another, for who hasn't wanted to escape from someone or something at sometime?

All too often we hear about young people who run away from home, who get lost in the subcultures of our society, who become addicted to drugs. But what about their parents who are "running away"? Alcoholism is on the rise. Excessive drinking is a form of "running." The "Happy Hour" is a fast lap around the track. Even addiction to prescription drugs of one type or another is a way of "jogging" loose from the mounting pressures of life.

And what about the rising number of broken marriages? That

too might be a way of escape. We don't like pain of any kind. We take aspirin for our headaches, soothing medicines for our stomachaches, and painkilling tablets for whatever else that might hurt us. And that's OK. But it's typical of our desire to be relieved of pain.

Rather than working through problems that produce emotional pain, some individuals decide that it's time to leave, it's time to run. "Who wants to take this verbal abuse?" "Who wants to struggle with this emotionally charged problem?" "Why not leave?" And so they do leave. Thousands leave every year.

In many ways, "running away" is a spiritual affair. When Cain got crossways with God and murdered his brother Abel, he became a "runaway." In fact, the land of Nod to which he fled actually means "Place of Wandering."

People who haven't found peace with God are wanderers, too, roaming from place to place, from person to person, from one kick to another, from one experience to another, looking for peace of mind. Isn't that a common story?

Maybe it's time that we faced up to life. Maybe it's time that we realized that life was never intended to be a rose garden where we could dream our way into fantasy land. Maybe it's time that we turned to God for inner peace, forgiveness, wholeness, and purpose for our lives. Or would you rather run away?

**Where could I go to escape from you?**
**Where could I get away from your presence?**
**If I went up to heaven, you would be there;**
**if I lay down in the world of the dead, you would be there.**
**If I flew away beyond the east**
**or lived in the farthest place in the west,**
**you would be there to lead me,**
**you would be there to help me.**
**(Ps. 139:7-10, TEV)**

Is there anybody here who has not said, I will have no more of it; I will break its bands asunder; I will cast away its cords and

> have my own way? Have we ever entirely succeeded? There is something there we cannot be rid of. We have to deal with it one way or another, either to follow it, be true to it, or else be haunted by it. There is something in us that holds on and follows after and calls back.[8]

*Lord, I find it easy to want to run away. Sometimes the pressures are so great that I don't think I can stand another day. Sometimes your will is so heavy that I feel I will break under the stress. Help me to know, dear Lord, that you'll never put more on me than I can bear, and what's more, you have promised to help me to bear it. So why should I run away. Give me your help—today. Amen.*

## The Sign on the Door

I saw the sign hanging from the doorknob. It read: PLEASE DO NOT DISTURB. The occupants wanted privacy, rest, and to be left alone. I have felt that way at times, haven't you? Haven't you wanted to hang a sign on the doorknob of your life—a sign that advised people just to let you alone?

Life gets hectic. It spins around and around, and we get caught up in its whirlwind. We hardly have time to think. We struggle to keep our sanity.

At such times, we might want to withdraw from everything—to back off, so to speak. We want to hide in our little "rooms" and say to the world what one person had placed on her tombstone:

> Don't bother me now, don't bother me ever,
> I want to be dead forever and forever.

Of course, there are other ways we don't want to be disturbed. We've all had certain situations which we wish we might be able to freeze and preserve forever. Good health, tranquil family relationships, communities secure and peaceful—these are examples of that which we wish not to be disturbed. A child at a carnival, an athlete having an outstanding game, the feeling that God is in control—good feelings, good experiences.

But if we live, disturbance will come—change will come. People will leave us, and we will leave people. Health will change, and we'll battle with illness. People will die, people who mean much to us. Nothing stays the same. You don't; I don't. Only God does.

One day God said to his people as they camped somewhere between Egypt and the Promised Land, "You have stayed long enough at this mountain. Break camp and move on" (Deut. 1:6*b*-7*a*, TEV).

For a year they had enjoyed the beautiful sunrises and sunsets at their mountain retreat. Their legs were resting from the long, arduous journey. And now, their rest was over. Their peace was disturbed.

But what if it had not been disturbed? Would they have been content to stay where they were? Would they have ever moved toward their goal? Probably not. And yet, the mountain was not the Promised Land. It was not their final destination.

When God disturbs our peace, it isn't that he is a "pest" who delights in watching others suffer. It's because he wants us to move on to something better, something more wonderful, something greater than anything we have ever known.

Think of it this way: If God never disturbed us, would we ever turn to Christ? Probably not. So he makes us discontented with what we have, with where we are, with who we are. He makes us restless, so that we will turn to the One who gives us rest, real rest.

The next time God disturbs your "sleep," don't say, "Why are you bothering me? Why are you disturbing me?" Instead, say, "Lord, what would you have me to do?" You'll be glad you did.

> **Like an eagle that stirs up its nest,**
> **That hovers over its young,**
> **He spread His wings and caught them,**
> **He carried them on his pinions.**
> **(Deut. 32:11, NASB)**

In his autobiography, *With Christ At Sea*, Frank Bullen told how he often stood on the deck of his ship and listened to the church bells. He said he listened

> with a deep yearning in him for something—he didn't know what—with a hunger which was neither physical nor mental, but deeper than both. For years it had disquieted him. All sorts of things wakened this hunger in him—the sight of a church steeple, the tone of an organ. Nature stirred it—the smell of the woods, the song of the bird, the silent, majestic movement of the stars at sea. Until one day the pent-up feelings of years broke loose and he felt overtaken by something that had pursued him all his days, some deep out there calling to the deep in him.[9]

*Lord, in my mind, I know all of that. I know that life is movement, change, disturbance. I know there are goals I have not reached, promised lands I have not claimed. When I become too comfortable with something that is less than your best for me, disturb me and direct me. But Lord, a little rest here and there would be appreciated too. Thank you for the disturbance and the rest. Amen.*

## Butterflies

Have you ever tried to catch a butterfly? If you have a net, you're in luck, but if you're trying to catch one with your hands, you might as well forget it.

Butterflies are elusive. They flit from place to place, change direction in an instant, swoop low to the ground or climb over treetops, and just about the time you think you have one trapped, it quickly eludes your darting fingers.

Contentment is somewhat like a butterfly. It too is hard to catch, and maybe even more difficult to hold. Some people say they have it, but many people say they don't.

Not everyone is certain about what it is. Some say it is based upon your possessions. But is it? If it is, why aren't all rich people content? And why are some poor people content?

A young man of great wealth asked Jesus what he could do to

receive the quality of life that Jesus seemed to be experiencing. Why should he want more? He was rich. He was young. He had political power. But he didn't have contentment.

Some say that contentment is based upon what you receive. But is it? The Dead Sea receives rivers of water from a number of streams, but it gives out no water except that which it loses by evaporation. Nothing lives in its waters. It's all right to receive, but it's better to give. Jesus said it was, and it really is. Givers seem to be happier people than receivers.

Contentment? Well, some say it is based upon freedom from struggle or pain. But is it? Would life be better if it were all sun and no rain? If all the colors were red or blue or yellow, would we not miss the indigo and violet? In fact, black is beautiful, too, and brown and orange and green. We need all the colors, don't we? Just like we need some pain. Just like we need some sadness. Just like we need some losses here and there to make us appreciate the good that we have.

Some say that contentment is based upon the hope that we have in this life. But is it? Life can be very disappointing. It can even be tragic. Paul said, "If in this life only we have hope in Christ, we are of all men most miserable" (1 Cor. 15:19). The really contented people are those who know there is more to our existence than this life. There is heaven. There is eternity. There is God.

Whatever it is, contentment is not something you automatically have. Paul said, "I have learned, in whatsoever state I am, therewith to be content" (Phil. 4:11). "I have learned . . ." Learning comes from study. Learning comes from experience. We must learn how to treat the good and accept the bad. We must learn how to allow God to win the victory through us. Contentment is something God wants each of us to have. Real contentment is his gift to us.

I wish for you "contentment." But more than that, I wish for you "Jesus." When you have him in your life, you'll be on your way toward the discovery of contentment. You really will.

**They think that religion is a way to become rich. Well,**

**religion does make a person very rich, if he is satisfied with what he has. What did we bring into the world? Nothing! What can we take out of the world? Nothing! So then, if we have food and clothes, that should be enough for us. (1 Tim. 6:5*b*-8, TEV)**

> . . . what this universe is bent on producing here is not primarily a good world but a good man, a complete person. What God is making here is man. All the rest is scenery. There is no permanence in anything except in the soul that is made in the struggle. Man is the end product of creation.[10]

*Your will, Lord, following your will for my life—that's where it is! That's how it comes. Even now as I recall the times when I have felt the best about myself and about life, I remember that it has been those times when I felt that I was the most surrendered to you. Help me to learn from Jesus the way to be content. Help me to learn by experience how to be content. For this, I pray. Amen.*

## Making the Most of a Miss

Recently, our daughter had to fill out a questionnaire in which she was to select the classes she would like to attend in the next school year. But it wasn't all that simple. She had to put her second and third choices in case a class or some classes should already be filled.

Isn't that like life? Do you always get your "first" choice, or are you forced to take the second, third, or even fourth best? It would be nice if we could plan the agenda of our futures, if we could have our first choices in health, happiness, fulfillment, and so forth. Which one of us wouldn't be delighted to program for himself or herself that which would seem to be the ideal for a happy and meaningful existence?

But unfortunately, life doesn't work that way. We don't always get our "first choices." In fact, some of the things we get, were we to have the privilege of choosing, we wouldn't select at any number. They're thrust upon us. We're not even consulted about them. Our opinions are not regarded at all.

Obviously, we could be petulant and kick up our heels against the unfairness we feel we have experienced. We could hurl our accusations against our oppressors and even against God. We could say, "Since I didn't get my first or second choices, I don't want any. I won't even go to your stupid old school!" Or, to put it in another context, we could say, "Since I didn't get the job I wanted, I won't take any job. Since I didn't get the car I wanted, I won't buy any car." And on it could go.

The alternative to that is to take what one does get and look for a few surprises here and there. I think I can honestly say about my life that I have not always had my first, second, or even third choices in some situations. But it has been in the "leftovers" that I have found some of my greatest pleasure.

One woman, speaking about her rejection as a child, said, "Don't weep for me. I needed those experiences, for you see, they brought me to God." I wonder how many experiences have brought us to God.

The Taj Mahal, one of the most beautiful buildings in the world, is a product of pain, the sorrow of death which a man suffered. And some of the most beautiful songs that have been written were composed by men and women who were shattered by the loss of their first or second choices.

If you miss what you consider to be the best, why not try to make the most of a miss? God can help us to do that if we would surrender ourselves and our situations to him. Paul put it this way: "I know what it is to be in need and what it is to have more than enough. I have learned this secret, so that anywhere, at any time, I am content, whether I am full or hungry. . . . I have the strength to face all conditions by the power that Christ gives me" (Phil. 4:12-13, TEV).

That's the kind of attitude it will take if we are to make the most of a miss. It certainly beats quitting, doesn't it? Let's give it a try.

**Some were living in gloom and darkness,**
**prisoners suffering in chains.**

**.................................................**

**Then in their trouble they called to the Lord,**
**and he saved them from the distress.**

**.................................................**

**They must thank the Lord for his constant love,**
**for the wonderful things he did for them.**
**(Ps. 107:10,13,15, TEV)**

> On the formal level we classify events as being good or bad according to whether they were favourable to us or not. This is, of course, true. But on a deeper level, it is our underlying attitude to them that matters. We suffer an injustice; if we are made rebellious by it, it arouses evil in our hearts; if we can bear it unselfishly, it becomes, on the contrary, the occasion of a rich inner experience. We win a success: if it provokes us to pride, it is fatal for us; if it makes us work even harder, it is good. Seen from this angle, objectively, good events are sometimes revealed as harmful, while others, thought to be bad, turn out to have good results. Everything can be useful, and everything can be harmful, according to the spirit in which a person reacts.[11]

*Lord, help me to learn that many things cannot be judged at the time they happen. Some things that may seem good at the time may not be so good after all, and some things that seem devastating at the time could have good results. Teach me the art of surrendering my life and all that I am and have to you. Help me to know that in Calvary, you made the most of what looked like a miss. Amen.*

## From Here to There

One day the noted musician, Pablo Casals, was practicing the musical scales on his cello. A visitor asked, "Do you really have to practice the scales?" The musician responded: "Ah, my friend, the whole program in playing the cello is how to get from one note to the next." Getting from here to there is also the whole problem of life.

Some people struggle to get from one day to the next, and some even struggle to get from morning to evening. There are even those of us who struggle to get from one hour to the next or one minute to the next.

Casals had done something very interesting insofar as his visitor was concerned. He, the master cellist, was actually doing what one might expect a beginner to do. He was practicing the musical scale, going from one note to the next. He was familiarizing himself with the basic fundamentals of his trade. That might be good advice for us all.

Some of us have a tendency to make life much more complicated than it already is. We think in terms of symphonies when we should be thinking of one note at a time. We anticipate too many tomorrows, and thus we often do a poor job with today. Anxiety can overload the system. Too many thoughts can do for the mind what too many electrical connections can do for a fuse. We find ourselves sitting in darkness when we should be walking in the light. We worry and fret when we should be calm. One note to the next, one note at a time, that is what the renowned musician was doing. That is what you and I should learn to do, too.

There is a word from the Lord that speaks to that issue. "As thy days, so shall thy strength be" (Deut. 33:25). It was another way of saying that we should play one note at a time—live one day at a time. We don't have tomorrow's allotment of strength ahead of time. We only have today's. And didn't Jesus say something about "our *daily* bread"? (Matt. 6:11, author's italics). Why then are we trying to overload ourselves by asking for more than God said would be available to us?

If our song is going to be sung tomorrow, we will need the strength and wisdom to play the chords. Far too many of us lose life's music because we fail to live one day at a time. We fail to play one note at a time.

The secret is in learning how to trust in God. For tomorrow and its needs, we must not pray. Just for today—that's what we need—

strength for today. We must learn how to surrender all of our tomorrows to God and walk with him one day at a time.

"One note at a time." That's a good way to get music from a cello. It's also a good way to get a song in one's heart. "As thy days, so shall thy strength be." That's the best way I know for getting from here to there.

> **But those who trust in the Lord for help**
> **will find their strength renewed.**
> **They will rise on wings like eagles;**
> **they will run and not get weary;**
> **they will walk and not grow weak.**
> **(Isa. 40:31, TEV)**

> We are absolutely in the hand of God, and the supreme folly of this twentieth century is the folly of thinking that because we have acquired a certain amount of knowledge of the laws of God, we are independent of Him. We cannot live for a day without Him. Nothing would continue were it not sustained and kept going by God. "Give us this day our daily bread." It is a good thing for us at least once a day, but the oftener the better, to remind ourselves that our times, our health, and our very existence, are in His hands.[12]

*Lord, I confess that sometimes life gets to be very heavy. I wonder if I'll ever "fly again." Walking is even hard to do. Putting one foot in front of another is quite a chore. Teach me the art of living one day at a time. Lord, help me to trust myself, my day, and my days to you. Keep me in your care, I pray. Amen.*

# 2

# FREE

To most people in the world, *free* is a word about which they know little, if anything. Some words are like that. We can spell them. We can pronounce them. We can define them. But we don't experience them. "Ye shall know the truth, and the truth shall make you free" (John 8:32). Is true freedom only a dream and nothing more? Is it a thought and little else? Many of us are slaves—if not to governments, then slaves to self, to habits, to sins, to our appetites. Can anyone set us free? "If the Son therefore shall make you free, ye shall be free indeed" (John 8:36). We have not received God's best until his Son sets us free.

## Learning to Be Free

Many of us are fighting with a problem, and unfortunately we're losing the fight. It's a problem that is within ourselves, within our minds, within our spirits. It's a problem that concerns our abilities and limitations.

We're anxiety ridden and sometimes depressed because of our failure to cope with this problem. We build up deep resentments and even hatreds. Much peace of mind is lost. We can't sleep at night, and we might even be developing needless ulcers because of this difficulty.

Everyone has limitations. People are not created equal. Some have more talent than others. Some have more opportunities than others. And some do more with the talents and opportunities they have than others do.

But we live with two words that begin with the letter "a"—*awareness* and *ambition*. We're "aware" of others, what they do, and we have "ambition," the desire to excel, the drive to be successful.

Awareness of others causes us to compare ourselves with them. Ambition causes us to try to equal or excel them. There are times when that may be possible. Others bring out the best in us. Competition with them creates a greater desire and drive within us. But there may be times when it frustrates us and destroys our peace of mind and tranquility.

A few years ago our children were swimming in a motel pool. They were diving from the diving board and having a good time in the deeper water. A young boy, who was about the age of our son, watched them. They were having fun, and he wanted to do the same. *Awareness* and *ambition.* Those two words nearly caused him to lose his life. He dove from the diving board into the deep water, but he couldn't swim. A lifeguard rescued him. Had he been able to accept himself, his ability, and his limitation, he would not have had a narrow escape with death.

The psalmist said, "The Lord preserveth the simple" (Ps. 116:6). Perhaps that statement has several meanings, but here is one way it can be understood. God gives peace and joy to those who cease living on the basis of what they would like to be and do and who start living on the basis of what they are and can do.

The plea for simpler living starts with self-assessment. Knowing one's self, knowing one's limitations, and being satisfied to do the very best with what one can do is the beginning of our search for personal freedom. Learning to be free—we'd better learn before we destroy ourselves.

**And because of God's gracious gift to me I say to every one of you: Do not think of yourself more highly than you should. Instead, be modest in your thinking, and judge yourself according to the amount of faith that God has given you. (Rom. 12:3, TEV)**

> The spiritual life can be lived in as many ways as there are people. What is new is that we have moved from the many things to the kingdom of God. What is new is that we are set free from the compulsions of our world and have set our hearts on the only necessary thing. What is new is that we no longer experience the many things, people, and events as endless causes for worry, but begin to experience them as the rich variety of ways in which God makes his presence known to us.[1]

*God of peace, give me your peace today. Help me to learn to be accountable to you and you alone. Lord, if I can just be the person you want me to be, I will have no need of comparing myself to others. Set me free I pray. Amen.*

# The Choice

As we make our journey through life, there are people who make a profound impact on our lives. Some affect us positively. Some affect us negatively. There are some whom we might wish we had never met or known. There are some we wish we could have known sooner.

Martha made a good impression on me. For more than twenty-five years, she was handicapped as a paraplegic following an automobile accident. But while her body had no coordination, her mind was unaffected by the tragedy. She had a keen sense of humor, a deep appreciation of life and people, and a way about her that endeared her to others.

One day she and I were talking about choices that people make. I shall never forget what she said. "When I awaken in the morning, I have two choices to make. Will I be happy? or will I be sad? Only a fool would choose to be sad, so I choose to be happy." One's attitude toward life is a choice.

Martha was a prisoner of a chair. She could not move it; someone had to help her. She was a prisoner of a body that could not feed itself. Others had to lift the food to her mouth. She was a prisoner of a bed from which she could not rise; someone had to help her move from it to her chair. For more than twenty-five years following the accident, she did not know a single day without some form of physical discomfort in addition to her paralysis.

Today, as I remember Martha, I remember a "free" person. The fences that surround so many of us did not enclose her life. The things that seem as if they have "life and death" dimensions to us did not hold her captive. She was free in a way that I want to be free, too. She held no bitterness toward God or the accident that took her out of life's mainstream. Though her body was immobilized, her mind was free to roam. She grew mentally and spiritually during those years after the accident. She developed a deeper appreciation for people. She gave more to others than others could possibly have given to her. Martha was a winner.

So many people are not free. Degrading habits, bad attitudes, bitterness, hatred, and other dreaded diseases of the mind have captured them. They are being held as prisoners in a sort of solitary confinement. They seem not to be able to escape.

What was the secret of Martha's freedom? Faith in God. Martha believed that God could work "*all things* . . . together for good" (Rom. 8:28). Her peace of mind was a direct result of the surrender of her will to God.

No, it isn't the circumstances we have in life that imprison us; it's the way we respond to those circumstances. Martha chose God. She chose freedom. Which will you choose—the problem? or the Answer?

**Get rid of all bitterness, passion, and anger. No more shouting or insults, no more hateful feelings of any sort. Instead, be kind and tender-hearted to one another, and forgive one another, as God has forgiven you through Christ. (Eph. 4:31-32, TEV)**

> One has but to recall Milton's blindness, Beethoven's deafness, Coleridge's headaches, to remember what grandeur humanity has often achieved in spite of difficulties. Dostoevsky, who spent several years in the lonely exile of Siberia before becoming a great novelist, said that 'suffering is the sole origin of human consciousness.' Suffering, unless we abjure it and retreat from it, causes us to sharpen our wits, discipline our talents, and develop our possibilities.[2]

*Lord, I thank you for the "Marthas" of life who teach us so much about your adequacy to meet all our needs. When I am tempted to give in to a spirit of despair and hopelessness, help me to know that I could just as easily choose you. And if I choose you, I choose peace and joy. Lord, help me to make the right choice. Amen.*

## The General Store

Some of us at some time in our past have had experiences with the good old "general store." Those stores had just about everything—clothes, hardware, food, ice cream, farm supplies, even a small pharmacy.

I have always enjoyed looking through those stores, but I would have hated to have tried to manage one of them. Where would you find things? How could you begin to take an inventory? There were so many items in such a small area.

Then the thought has occurred to me that some of us are human forms of the "general store." There is so much going on in our lives, so many obligations and requirements. We belong to this organization and that. We have our days and nights committed to someone or something. The "aisles" of our lives are littered with the demands made upon our time and energy. We're not free to think, to be still, to relax.

As a result, we hardly enjoy doing the things we do. Everything is a drudgery. We must force ourselves to participate in all that is expected of us. Husbands and wives wave to each other in passing—if they see each other at all. Children hardly recognize the sounds of their parents' voices, and parents know little, if anything, about their children's friends or life-styles.

If you're a "general store" type individual, what can you do about it? Some feel as if they would like to throw the whole mess in the ocean and run away from it all. "Stop the world, I want to get off!" they shout. But we can't stop the world. We've got to learn to live within it. How can we?

To begin with we might have to do some thorough "housecleaning." We must decide what is the most important item in our "store" and work down to the least important. Some things must stay, and some things must go.

When we set our priorities there will be some hard choices that will follow. We must say no to some people, some events, and some things. That might not make us popular, but it could help save our marriages, our children, our sanity, and even our lives.

In one of his stories, Jesus described the "overcrowded" life by comparing it to ground where weeds and thorns were in abundance. The good seed was planted, and it managed to grow. But it didn't grow to the fullest of its potential. There were too many weeds to allow for that. The cluttered condition of the soil soon choked it out. The farmer missed the kind of harvest that could have fed him and others.

There are many people who are missing peace of mind because of their cluttered lives. They're also missing God. They have no time for worship, Bible study, or prayer. They have no time to develop their spirits and friendships. They have no time for the finer things in life. And who loses? We know who loses.

Maybe it's time for some of us to do some housecleaning. Perhaps it's time to simplify life. Some choices must be made. I strongly urge you to choose God first, and other choices must fit into that one. If we're going to experience inner peace and freedom from frustration, we've got to "clean up the store."

**There were so many people coming and going that Jesus and his disciples didn't even have time to eat. So he said to them, "Let us go off by ourselves to some place where we will be alone and you can rest a while." (Mark 6:31, TEV)**

> For some people the hardest words in the English language are *I'm sorry*. For me it is the word *no*. I would like to be able to say yes to everyone and everything, but obedience to Christ requires me at times to say no. Like the gardener pruning the vine, I must constantly prune away unnecessary activities if new life is to spring forth. Otherwise, I will droop under heavy vines with little productiveness, frustration, and fatigue the inevitable result.[3]

*Lord, I pray for wisdom to know your essential will for my life. I pray for strength to be able to say no when necessary. I ask that you will give me the joy of your blessed quietness in the midst of all that whirls about me. Help me to "clean up the store." In Jesus' name, I pray. Amen.*

## How Hungry Are You?

The story has been told about a young man who approached Gautama Buddha seeking the true way of life, the path of deliverance. Buddha led him down to a river, and the young man assumed he must go through some rite of purification. They entered the water together and waded until the water level was quite deep. At that point, Buddha placed his hands on the shoulders of the young man and gently pushed him under the water.

He held him there until the inquirer began to get restless. The lad began to squirm and wanted air to breathe, but Buddha held him firmly under the water. Finally, in desperation the young man broke from Buddha's grasp and emerged from the water gasping for air.

When he asked about the meaning of such a lengthy submerging, Buddha responded by asking, "When you were under the water, what did you want more than anything?" "Air," was the quick reply. "Very well," said Buddha, "when you want salvation as much as you wanted air, you shall have it."

There's a great deal of truth in that statement. All over the world there are people who are looking for meaning to life. Boredom and emptiness characterize their thinking and living. They would love to be free from the abysmal feeling of meaninglessness. Unfortunately, many of them do not want this freedom enough to pay the price required.

Another young man on another day approached Jesus and asked for much the same thing the young man asked of Buddha. "What . . . must I do, to have eternal life?" (Matt. 19:16, RSV). He was rich and powerful, one of Palestine's young aristocrats. Jesus asked him to sell what he had and give the proceeds to the poor. He wouldn't do it, and we are told that "he went away sorrowful" (v. 22). Why wasn't he angry? Why didn't he say, "Man, you must be stupid if you think I would do something like that?" Why didn't he laugh at Jesus?

Maybe it was because he knew that Christ was right. His money, power, and possessions had such a strong hold on him that he could not surrender them. Those were the true "lord" of his life that held him captive. He did not want to release them and become obedient to the lordship of Christ. As a consequence, he missed eternal life. He missed the ultimate freedom.

Jesus wasn't inferring that money is bad, that power is bad, that political leadership is bad. Not at all! That wasn't the issue. The issue was—"Are you willing to pay the price for the freedom which you seek?"

The same is still true. God has eternal life which he wants to give to us. He has the gift of joy which he desires to present us. The question is: Do we want it badly enough to make the surrender that is required? The question is: How hungry are we?

**I alone know the plans I have for you, plans to bring you prosperity and not disaster, plans to bring about the future you hope for. Then you will call to me. You will come and pray to me, and I will answer you. You will seek me, and you will find me because you will seek me with all your heart. (Jer. 29:11-13, TEV)**

> Since God's prescription for genuine living revolves around the verb "to give" instead of "to get," then to give of oneself is a happy, though sometimes painful experience. Self-giving is our desperate need! So long as one is prosperous enough to pick up a checkbook and write out full payment for all his desires, he will not know the genuine joy of giving a part of the checkwriter.[4]

*Lord, I say I want you. I say that I want you more than anything or anyone else in the whole world. Sometimes I sing, "I'd rather have Jesus than silver or gold." Would I? Lord, you know my heart. Help me to really mean what I say and sing. Help me to be hungry—for you. Amen.*

## Trapped

Have you ever felt trapped—I mean, really trapped? Have you experienced a time in your life when things looked bleak and despairing? Perhaps you were caught in a dilemma that seemed hopeless to you. Maybe you felt hemmed in by circumstances over which you had little, if any, control. You simply had to sit and watch it happen.

It is that sinking feeling the spectator has when he looks at the scoreboard and recognizes that the game is nearly over, and his team is behind in the score. What can one do but sit and wait?

Perhaps it is a financial crisis, when the debts seem to mount and the resources dwindle. Maybe it's the time when the doctor solemnly tells the family, "We've done all we can do for your loved one."

Certainly there are times in our lives when we really are trapped. In such times, we don't ask for justice; we beg for mercy. We want an invasion from beyond the sphere of the normal. We want miracles.

One day the entire population of Israel felt trapped. The proverbial "roof" had fallen in on them. Although it was nothing more than they had a right to expect, it nonetheless was no easier to bear.

Sixty-seven years passed—years in which the people had not seen their homeland—long years, wasted years. They were being held as prisoners of war. For most of them, the thought of ever going home again had long since been forgotten. In despair they bowed their heads. In hopelessness they watched the time tick away.

They were trapped, but God wasn't. God never is. One thing after another happened until finally the people were set free. They were free to leave, to go home, home to their hills and seacoasts. It was like the team making a dramatic comeback and winning the game. It was like the doctor saying, "We don't know what has happened, but the patient has made remarkable strides toward recovery."

One man among that group was a poet, a poet who loved God and never ceased serving him even in the midst of the gloomy circumstances. He sat down and began writing the expression of his joy: "Bless the Lord, O my soul; and all that is within me, bless his holy name. Bless the Lord, O my soul, and forget not all his benefits" (Ps. 103:1-2). It was the expression of spontaneous joy.

You and I would do well to learn from that story. No matter how "trapped" we may feel ourselves to be at times, God is not trapped. He knows where we are. He knows what we need. We must learn to trust him and not be afraid.

No situation is hopeless until God gives up. I've got a strong feeling that he hasn't given up yet. He's still working on our freedom.

> **Proclaim with me the Lord's greatness;**
> **let us praise his name together!**
> **I prayed to the Lord, and he answered me;**
> **he freed me from all my fears.**
> **(Ps. 34:3-4, TEV)**

O, dear God—
It comes to me
With sweet and gentle relief
That this thing in my life
Which I can't possibly handle
Is the one thing above all
That You *can* handle.
You can handle it totally
And You can handle it now.

*"Yes, dear child—*
*Now let me!"*[5]

*Lord, I know the feeling. I know it well. I know the sense of desperation that people feel when they're trapped by some circumstance over which they have no control. It's a terrible feeling. Right now, Lord, help me to allow you the freedom of setting me free. Help me to cooperate with the rescue efforts. Amen.*

## Just Once More

Everyone has some temptation that more often than not will get the best of him. Usually after giving in to such a temptation, the individual will feel very sorry about his weakness. He might mentally "kick himself in the shins" and say, "That's it! No more. I won't do that again as long as I live." Remember—that's the feeling one has *immediately* after the failure, after the sin has been committed. There is guilt. There is sorrow. And there might be a renewed dedication to be strong and not give in to the temptation again.

Later, the temptation returns. It always returns. Why shouldn't it? If it won the last time, why not return to the scene of the crime and see if there is another victory to be won?

Most of our temptations are not too creative. That is, we may not have multiple weaknesses where the power of the tempter is strong. The devil usually concentrates on a few chosen areas of our lives. And that's our problem. We keep getting pounded at the same old spots. We wish he would let us alone in those areas and try something new for a change. But he doesn't. He knows where we're weak, and he'll go back to the same spot nearly every time.

When the temptation returns, perhaps our first impulse is to resist it. "Oh, no, you don't. Not this time. You're not going to get me into that mess again!" That's our *first* impulse. If we could just fortify ourselves and "hang in there," we might win. But many times we don't. Something within us seems to whisper—"Just once more, just this time. This is the last time for sure. After this time, there will be no other times." That sounds pretty good to us. What have we done?

First, we have eased the tension that comes to the mind and body whenever a temptation is presented to us. We have eased the pressure of the temptation mainly because we have given in to it.

Second, we have eased our consciences by telling ourselves, "This is the last time—ever!" So the body and mind are comfortable with the decision, and the conscience is somewhat comfortable. Therefore, it must be all right.

That kind of compromise is bad enough, but it usually doesn't stop at that point. The next time the temptation comes, we are urged to repeat the process—"Just once more—this *really is* the last time!" So what else is new?

Sooner or later we have got to learn that no temptation will be successfully resisted until we make a decisive and final answer—no! But even then, we'd do well to put something good into our minds as quickly as possible. It isn't enough to say no to evil; we must learn to say yes to some good thing.

Admittedly, overcoming evil in any of its forms is difficult, but God can help us to gain the victory. James encouraged us to "Resist the Devil, and he will run away from you. Come near to God, and he will come near to you" (Jas. 4:7, TEV). Try that the next time a temptation comes your way.

**Forgive us the wrongs we have done,**
**as we forgive the wrongs that others have done to us.**
**Do not bring us to hard testing,**
**but keep us safe from the Evil One.**
**(Matt. 6:12-13, TEV)**

Is life hard and difficult?
Are your burdens too heavy to bear?
Remember that the unseen, but very real God was himself a man once.
He knew temptation.
He knew difficulty.
He knew ingratitude.
He knew disappointment.
He knew the hearts of men, without illusion and without cynicism.
So he understands your heart and mine—fully.
He knows, you know.[6]

*Father in heaven, right now in the quietness of this moment, I am strong. I feel that no temptation could overcome me. But that's not my problem. My problem is that which I must face later, when I'm not in worship, or prayer, or studying your word. Temptation seems to slip up on me. Lord, help me not to take your strength for granted. Help me not to underestimate the power of the Evil One. Give me the power to win. Amen.*

# The Leaf

In the late fall one year, a young boy was seen straddling the limb of a tree in his front yard. Clumsily, he was trying to tie a string to the stem of a leaf and the leaf onto a twig on which it was growing. An elderly man stopped to watch the procedure. Inquisitively he asked, "Why are you trying to tie the leaf to the tree?" Through his tears, the boy made his response. He told the man about his little sister who was near death. The doctor had just told the family that "ere the last leaf shall fall from the tree in the front yard, she will be gone." "Don't you see, Mister, I don't want her to ever be gone. That's why I'm tying this leaf to the tree."

When winter comes, the leaf will fall from the tree. Even if the lad had been successful in tying the leaf to the tree, he could not have bound life and held it in the body of his younger sister.

Change is a fact of life. An old philosopher once noted: "You never see the same river twice." The water is constantly moving out and new water is taking its place. Even the shape and form of the water is not the same. We live in a sea of change.

Perhaps many of us can identify with the young child. There are situations from which we don't want to be free. There are relationships we enjoy. There are people who bring us great fulfillment. We would like to "tie these leaves to the tree" and keep them forever. In time, however, all things change. Health changes. Abilities change. Opportunities change. Any casual look at an old family album will reveal remarkable changes—even in us.

What shall we do about change? We can become depressed and resentful. We can deny ourselves deep relationships with others for fear of the pain that losing them might bring. We can try to keep our children tied to us, dependent upon us physically and emotionally. We could try to "tie the leaves to the trees" of our lives. The outward form might remain, but what good is a brown leaf with a string tied to it? What have we got if we have no life?

What shall we do about change? We can pretend as if it will never happen. We can pretend as if it hasn't ever happened. We can try to deny our age, our limitations, our existing circumstances. Of course, if we do that, we can become rather paranoid and neurotic. The leaf won't live just because there's a string around its stem.

What shall we do about change? Why not accept it as a fact of life? Why not approach every situation and circumstance as an opportunity for growth, for development? Why can't we realize that one reality is changeless—"God never changes." He who never changes can be with us to help us through all the changes of life. We can trust him, or we can try to tie leaves to trees.

**May the Lord our God be with us as he was with our ancestors; may he never leave us or abandon us; may he make us obedient to him, so that we will always live as he wants us to live, keeping all the laws and commands he gave our ancestors. (1 Kings 8:57-58, TEV)**

> God guides us, despite our uncertainties and our vagueness, even through our failings and mistakes. He often starts us off to the left, only to bring us up in the end to the right; or else he brings us back to the right, after a long detour, because we started off by mistake to the left in the belief that we were obeying him. He leads us step by step, from event to event. Only afterwards, as we look back over the way we have come and reconsider certain important moments in our lives in the light of all that has followed them, or when we survey the whole progress of our lives, do we experience the feeling of having been led without knowing it, the feeling that God has mysteriously guided us.[7]

*Lord, I admit it. There are places in my life I would like to freeze and hold forever—if I could. There are people who are very dear to me. I don't want to be free from their presence. There are situations and circumstances I like. I don't even want to think about them being changed. Father in heaven, help me to trust more completely in you so that when changes come, I will be strong. Free me from my fears, I pray. Amen.*

## On the Way to the Top

Have you ever noticed the "infighting" some people do as they try to reach the top? It would be humorous if it were not so tragic. Manipulation is a means by which some people "use" other people for their own gains. They're not really concerned about the other person—only about how the other person can help them to get where they want to be.

Closely akin to manipulation is exploitation. Perhaps that's a nastier word. It means "to take advantage of, to abuse." In either case, both methods are detestable. People are used as a means to an end—the end being the glorification of the person who is using or abusing the other.

In *King Lear,* Shakespeare gave us a moving piece of drama which illustrates the power plays people make to get what they want. The king was eighty years of age and wanted to divide his power with his daughters. He asked which of them loved him the most. Two of the daughters responded very aggressively. The third girl, Cordelia, was a quiet, almost timid child. But she loved her father deeply. In fact, she was the only one of the three who truly loved him for "his" sake. But since she did not openly declare her love, King Lear disinherited her and divided his power with his other daughters.

After the official action in which he divested himself of his power, he saw the error of his ways. The girls stripped him of his authority and laughed him to scorn. Cordelia, ever loving, sought him out, and Lear responded, "I am a very foolish fond old man/ . . . /Pray you now, forget and forgive." After the sisters had captured and imprisoned Lear and Cordelia, Lear says these words:

> We two alone will sing like birds i' the cage:
> When thou dost ask me blessing, I'll kneel down,
> And ask of thee forgiveness: so we'll live,
> And pray, and sing, and tell old tales,
> And laugh at gilded butterflies, and hear poor rogues
> Talk of court news; and we'll talk with them too,

> Who loses and who wins; who's in, who's out;
> And take upon's the mystery of things,
> As if we were God's spies.[8]

This man had to lose before he could win. He had to become a prisoner before he knew what it meant to be free from the power quest that consumes so many people. He became a king in the truest sense of the word only after he had lost his kingdom.

I suppose that as long as there are people, there will be those who want to reach the top. And maybe that's not bad. What is bad is the way some people try to achieve their goal. Jesus said, "What if you gain the whole world but lose your soul? What would a man give in exchange for his soul?" (Matt. 16:26, author's paraphrase). Someone said, "Be careful how you treat people on the way up. You might meet them again on the way down." It is better to be a prisoner and be free of an arrogant lust for power than to be a king whose head is too big to wear the crown.

**Don't think that there is no truth in the scripture that says, "The spirit that God placed in us is filled with fierce desires." But the grace that God gives is even stronger. As the scripture says, "God resists the proud, but gives grace to the humble." (Jas. 4:5-6, TEV)**

> Hear the words of Jesus: "A man's life consisteth not in the abundance of the things which he possesses." When all is said and done, the wisest will conclude that life is not measured by accumulation but by outlay, not by how much one has saved but how much he has wisely expended, not by distance traveled but by the route taken.[9]

*Father in heaven, help me to want to do the best I can with what you have given me. But Lord, spare me from that dreadful spirit of pride and arrogance that so often accompanies those who have achieved some goal in life. Help me to remember that the greatest One of all, your Son, never lost the sense of being a Servant to the least of us. Help me to be a servant, too. Amen.*

## Drifting and Dreaming

I wonder how many people sit back and dream a dream of freedom. There are those who go down to the seashore and look across the vast expanse of water and dream about the other side. Who might live there? What might life be like there?

There are those who are prisoners of their countries who dream a dream of freedom. Some of them, of course, could not handle the freedom if they were to get it. Freedom is an awesome responsibility. There are those who are behind bars who dream a dream of freedom.

There are those who are captives of diseased bodies who dream a dream of freedom. They wonder what it would be like to get one good breath of air without experiencing pain in breathing. They dream about having one good day with the ability to walk, to see, or hear. There are people longing to be free from some dreadful circumstance.

I suppose it's natural for most people to dream a dream of some kind of freedom, some type of liberation. Nearly all of us have something from which we would desire to be set free.

For some, that dream is a legitimate dream. That quest is an honorable quest. For others—well, it's unfortunate that we sometimes don't appreciate the good we have until we've lost it. Our restlessness and dreams for something different often cause us to cast aside that which we have in order to take hold of that which we wish we had. Isn't the grass always greener on the other side of the fence?

Jesus told us about a young man who dreamed a dream of freedom. The world was calling to him—the call of the wild. It wasn't long before the call became so loud that he could ignore it no longer. So off he went.

His dreaming made a drifter out of him—drifting from here to there. He dreamed of yet more worlds to conquer until at last he drifted into a "far country." It's terribly lonely in life's "far country." Our boy discovered it the hard way.

When he could take it no longer, he turned his head toward

home. His eyes looked beyond the mountains ahead of him—back through the years, far beyond his sins and mistakes—and he saw his "father's house." His homecoming ended in a beautiful celebration. It ended in real freedom.

It's OK to dream, to think big, to plan for something better. That's God's gift to you and me. If our dreams and plans are honorable, if they would make life better for ourselves and others, if they would honor God, then dream on! But don't stop with the dream. Start walking! And that will be your gift to God.

**This is what I will do in the last days, God says:**
**I will pour out my Spirit on everyone.**
**Your sons and daughters will proclaim my message;**
**your young men will see visions,**
**and your old men will have dreams. (Acts 2:17, TEV)**

> Not much happens without a dream. And for something great to happen, there must be a great dream. Behind every great achievement is a dreamer of great dreams. Much more than a dreamer is required to bring it to reality; but the dream must be there first.[10]

*Thank you, Lord, for the privilege of dreaming. Sometimes my dreams keep me going. Sometimes they inspire my actions. Sometimes they allow me to survive some rough seas. But, Lord, help me to dream your dreams for me and others. Help me to put my good dreams into action. Through Jesus Christ, I pray. Amen.*

## Why Wait?

Most of us spend a lot of time waiting. We wait in line at the ticket counter, the grocery store, and at the traffic lights. We wait for mail we wish would arrive. We wait for people to call us, to come to see us, to listen to us. We wait for comforting words, encouraging words, affirming words. We wait for God to answer a prayer here and there. We spend a lot of time waiting.

In many situations, we have no option. We must wait. We can't make something happen any faster than it is prepared to happen. Plants take time to grow. But so do lives. Too many mistakes have been made by people who decided not to wait, who decided to force the issue. Too many hearts have been broken.

I'm reminded of an area where we usually wait when in actuality we shouldn't wait. Ruth Harms Calkin said it this way: "Lord, I see with startling clarity that life is never long enough to put You off until tomorrow. . . . If I intend to walk with You tomorrow I must start today."[11]

Why do people wait for the best freedom one can experience? Why do we wait to commit our lives to God? Jesus promised us that if we would come to him he would give us rest and peace. Isn't that what we want? Why wait?

It seems a little absurd, yet it is true, that there are millions of people who are traveling through life carrying heavy burdens, burdens which they should not have to carry. We're like the farmer who was trudging along a country road one hot summer day. On his back he carried a hundred-pound sack of feed. His shoulders were stooped beneath the load. A friend drove by and offered him a ride in his truck. The driver was astonished when he peered through the rearview mirror. He saw his passenger sitting on the bed of the truck still carrying the sack of feed on his shoulders. Why hadn't he set it aside? Why did he continue to carry it?

But many of us are like that. God has promised to forgive our sins, yet we insist on carrying the heavy load of guilt. God has promised to supply us with the strength for living, yet we insist on carrying the burdens of anxiety and worry. God has promised to give us direction for our lives, yet we insist on making all of our decisions without consulting his leadership.

Waiting with patience might be the thing to do in some circumstances, but when it comes to receiving God's liberating love—why wait? God has a treasure he wishes us to have. He'll give it anytime we're ready to receive it. So why wait?

**So Jesus said to those who believed in him, "If you obey my teaching, you are really my disciples; you will know**

**the truth, and the truth will set you free." . . . "If the Son sets you free, then you will be really free." (John 8:31-32,36, TEV)**

> The man who keeps secret his most painful memories, his bitterest remorse and his most private convictions, must needs show also, in his whole demeanour and in all his relationships with other people, a certain reserve which they all intuitively feel. This reserve is contagious, and sets up an obstacle to the development of personal relationships. On the other hand, the liberation experienced by the man who has confessed his sins is also contagious, even if he says nothing about the burden that has been lifted from his shoulders.[12]

*Lord, I am so hungry and thirsty for the freedom Christ promised. Help me to learn to surrender all that I am and have to you. Help me to know that when you forgive, you forgive—permanently! Help me to know that when you promised to give me peace and rest, you really meant it. Lord, help me not to wait one more minute. I receive it now. In Jesus' name, I pray. Amen.*

# 3
# HELP

"Help" is a word we have heard; it's a word we have said. We shout it in times of despair—"Please help me!" We beg it in a time of perplexity—"Help me to understand!" We plead it in that time of weakness—"Help me!" All of us need help from time to time. Perhaps the help we need can be given by another person. Perhaps not. Maybe God alone can help us in our helplessness. "God is an ever-present help in the time of trouble" (see Ps. 46:1). "God helps those who help themselves," we have been told. Yes, and God helps those who can't help themselves. "Help" is a good word, especially when God gives it, especially when we receive it. God's best to you includes help. Trust him—and see!

## Thinking Too Much

Have you ever thought it would be possible to "think" too much? I know that those who are in positions of instructing others wish there would be much more thinking than there is.

But let me approach the subject in a different way. There are people who think too much. The human being has the capacity to do that, you know. We can "think the future" before the future. We can imagine what might be. Such is the cause for much of our worry and anxiety.

One day a man approached another man at a bus stop and asked for a match. The request was denied. Another man who overheard the request and knew it could have been granted asked why the stranger had not been given a match. The man responded, "Suppose I gave him a match. He would say, 'Nice day, isn't it?' And I would say, 'Yes, it is a nice day.' He would say, 'Who do you think will win the game this afternoon?' And I would say, 'Well, I'm not sure, who do you think will win?' He'd say, 'By the way, my name is, . . . what's your's?' I'd tell him my name, and he would ask if he could buy me a cup of coffee. While drinking coffee together, he'd ask me about my family. I'd tell him about my wife and daughter. He'd come to my house, meet my daughter, fall in love with her, marry her, and they'd have a house full of kids. I don't like kids. That's why I didn't give him a match." Now that's a classic case of "thinking too much."

Even though you and I might not be that ridiculous in our thinking, we still find ourselves thinking too much at times. That's why we're filled with anxieties and tensions. That's one of the reasons why we have nervous breakdowns and ulcerated stomachs. That's why people irritate us so easily.

Sooner or later we're going to have to learn how to do the best we can with the present moment and trust the future into the hands of a loving, caring, all-powerful God.

John said, "And we win the victory over the world by means of our faith. Who can defeat the world? Only the person who believes that Jesus is the Son of God" (1 John 5:4*b*-5, TEV).

Those people who believe those words enough to practice them in their daily living find an inner peace that some of the rest of us are missing. Certainly, it's possible for them to imagine what could happen, just as it's possible for us to imagine what the future could bring. Their secret is that they trust the future to God. They ask him for daily strength and guidance. They learn the art of depending upon the Lord for their help.

The next time someone asks you for the time of day, or a match, or anything, before you get to thinking too much about the future, remember that we have a Heavenly Father who can guide us when the future comes. Trust him and live the present moment to the fullest. You'll live better—for less!

**So do not start worrying: "Where will my food come from? or my drink? or my clothes?" (These are the things the pagans are always concerned about.) Your Father in heaven knows that you need all these things. (Matt. 6:31-32, TEV)**

> One of the most notable characteristics of worrying is that it fragments our lives. The many things to do, to think about, to plan for, the many people to remember, to visit, or to talk with, the many causes to attack or defend, all these pull us apart and make us lose our center. Worrying causes us to be "all over the place," but seldom at home. One way to express the spiritual crisis of our time is to say that most of us have an address but cannot be found there.[1]

*Lord, I confess to you that my mind works overtime sometimes. I think too much. I imagine things that could happen, and I worry about them. Lord, so much of my peace of mind is lost because I don't trust tomorrow to your loving care. Help me to surrender this day, yes, and all my days to you. Amen.*

## The Crippled Pup

A little crippled girl walked into the pet shop to choose her very own pet. There were so many animals that she didn't know which to choose. Finally, she settled for a small dog that had a lame leg. "Don't you want one that has four good legs?" her mother asked. "No," responded the child. "I want this one. I don't walk so good either."

Have you heard someone describe a situation in which you said to yourself, "I can identify with that?" Perhaps most of us could say that at one time or another. We've heard people describe situations or feelings, and we've wondered if they have been reading our mail. Their story sounds like our story. We can identify with it.

Speaking about the coming of Christ into the world, the Hebrews writer said, "He [Jesus] also says, . . . 'Here I am with the children that God has given me.' Since the children, as he calls them, are people of flesh and blood, Jesus himself became like them and shared their human nature. . . . And now he can help those who are tempted, because he himself was tempted and suffered" (Heb. 2:13-14,18, TEV). That's identification. That's the way God has identified with us.

One man said it this way, "Christ pitched his tent next to mine." I like that statement, for it is wonderfully suggestive of something important. His tent was set up beside my tent. When the storm struck during the night with its gusting winds and torrents of water, his tent took a beating just like mine did. When the lightning flashed and the sky was as bright as the middle of the day, his life was threatened just as much as mine. That's because he pitched his tent next to mine.

The Savior was not an absentee monarch who ruled from some ivory palace made of stone and steel. He walked the streets with the people, rubbing shoulders with them in the marketplace. He was well acquainted with their daily struggle for bread. He knew what it was to be tired and lonely, misunderstood and criticized. He pitched his tent next to mine.

His temptations were just as real as mine are, therefore he can identify with my anxiety, doubts, and fears. When the night was cold, his body felt it just like mine does. He pitched his tent next to mine.

It comforts me to know that the God whom I worship is not one who is unfamiliar with my struggles. He is not one who can't identify with my soul's anguish in the troubles of life. Alfred Lord Tennyson said, "I should be sorely afraid to live my life without God's presence, but to feel he is by my side just now as much as you are, that is the very joy of my heart." His tent is set beside mine.

Because he pitched his tent next to mine, I shall always have a good neighbor and friend, one who will gladly lend a helping hand. But more importantly than that, I have a Savior who has identified with me. He has come down to my level. Day by day, moment by moment, he is lifting me up to his level. Who could ask for anything more?

**Let us be bold, then, and say, "The Lord is my helper, I will not be afraid. What can anyone do to me?" (Heb. 13:6, TEV)**

Whereas patience is the mother of expectation, it is expectation itself that brings new joy to our lives. Jesus not only made us look at our pains, but also beyond them. . . . The paradox of expectation indeed is that those who believe in tomorrow can better live today, that those who expect joy to come out of sadness can discover the beginnings of a new life in the center of the old, that those who look forward to the returning Lord can discover him already in their midst.[2]

*And Lord, that's the good news to my heart today. The fact that you have promised to be with me today and tomorrow in the midst of the mess that I sometimes live in, that gives me courage and hope. It's a happy thought to know that some day I will be with you for all the eternal ages in heaven, but until then, I thank you for pitching your tent next to mine. It's good to have you so close. Amen.*

## I Just Can't . . .

Norman Vincent Peale wrote a popular book entitled *The Power Of Positive Thinking*. His thesis suggests that our minds have a tremendous way of controlling our success. People who think "positively" about themselves, their work, their future, and their God are more inclined to be successful than those who think negatively. I agree with him.

Someone needs to write a book entitled *The Power of Negative Thinking*. There may be more "negative" thinkers than there are "positive" thinkers. There may be more people who say, "I can't" than there are who say, "I can." We have a tendency to say about ourselves, "I'm not," instead of saying, "I am."

Some of us must think it is modest and appropriate to spend our time and energy depreciating ourselves instead of appreciating ourselves. We have reacted against the arrogant egotism of some by becoming faultfinding pessimists—especially when it comes to ourselves. We have heard that it is better to be humble than proud. (And it is.) The only problem is that we have gone to extremes to prove it.

Many of us are extremely critical of ourselves. We don't like our looks. We don't like our abilities. We don't like where we are in life. We don't like—and on and on the list goes. The power of "negative" thinking!

If we were only that way about ourselves, that would be bad enough, but our negativism tends to be applied to others as well, especially to those who might be significant individuals to us. Some husbands and wives, some mothers and fathers, some sons and daughters also become the victims of the "negative" thinker. They are periodically or constantly reminded of their failures while their successes are ignored.

Negative thinkers have a tendency to nag and criticize. Under the guise of trying to make another individual "all that he or she can be," they advise, push, ride a few backs, and "encourage," (which more often than not really means "discourage").

But it doesn't stop there either. We allow our "negative" thinking to send its tentacles like some giant octopus around other areas of life. We find fault with our business and professional leaders, our entertainers and politicians, our pastors, priests, and kings. No one seems to measure up to our high standards of excellence. We don't. Our loved ones don't. No one does. God doesn't even measure up. He forever seems to fail us. He doesn't answer our prayers. He doesn't bless us with the desires of our hearts. He allows things to come to us which we despise. He's the ever-absent help in the time of trouble.

The Proverb writer wisely said, "As [a man] thinketh in his heart, so is he" (Prov. 23:7). Negative thinkers create negative situations. They produce negative results. Negative thinkers exemplify little faith, hope, and love.

Paul said, "I can do all things through Christ which strengtheneth me" (Phil. 4:13). That means we can think "positively," doesn't it? What do you mean—"You can't"?

**In conclusion, my brothers, fill your minds with those things that are good and that deserve praise: things that are true, noble, right, pure, lovely, and honorable. Put into practice what you learned and received from me, both from my words and from my actions. And the God who gives us peace will be with you. (Phil. 4:8-9, TEV)**

> When the commandment [to love one's neighbor] is rightly understood, it also says the converse, "Thou shalt love thyself in the right way." If anyone, therefore, will not learn from Christianity to love himself in the right way, then neither can he love his neighbor. He may perhaps . . . cling to one or several other human beings, but this is by no means loving one's neighbor. To love oneself in the right way, and to love one's neighbor, are absolutely analogous concepts, and are at the bottom one and the same.[3]

*Lord, I must confess that it's easy to be a "negative" thinker. Maybe it's because I take the "positive" things for granted. Maybe it's because I am not realistic about myself and others. Father in heaven, help me to have a proper appreciation for myself so that I can value others more properly. Help me to know that you love me in spite of all that you know about me. Give me the power of "positive" thinking. In Jesus' name, I pray. Amen.*

## Decisions, Decisions

"Decisions, decisions, decisions. I would like to live one day without having to decide on something important," the woman desperately said. Which road shall I take? What meal should be prepared this evening? Should I take this promotion and move to another city, or should I remain where I am? What major shall I choose in school? Should we get married now? or should we wait a little longer? Decisions, decisions, decisions.

> There was an old sailor my grandfather knew
> Who had so many things which he wanted to do.
> That, whenever he thought it was time to begin,
> He couldn't because of the state he was in.

Who hasn't experienced it? One man called it "the midnight muddle of our minds." When asked by a psychiatrist if he had any difficulty in making up his mind, the young man responded, "Well, yes and no." I've been there. You've been there. Who hasn't? Is there any way we can be helped to make up our minds about important matters? There is.

Jeremiah said, "Stop at the crossroads; look for the ancient paths; ask, 'Where is the way that leads to what is good?' Then take that way, and you will find rest for yourselves" (see 6:16, author's paraphrase). What did he mean?

First, he advised us to stop at the crossroads. Stop at the point of the decision. Stop! Don't keep your engine running. Stop. Far too many people are so anxious to get somewhere that they fail to stop and think about their direction. Stop and talk with a trusted friend or counselor. Stop and pray. Seek the counsel of the Lord.

Second, look for the ancient paths. That is, let history help you make up your mind. Some things work. Some things don't work. Time is on the side of truth, goodness, and beauty. The Hitlers of the world have their day and then fade into oblivion. The pleasure seekers have their night of fun and then their pleasure leaves a bitter aftertaste.

Third, ask questions. "Where is the road that leads to what is good?" One must make a decision before he makes other decisions. That is, one must make a decision to reach a certain place before he decides on the route he will take. We must answer some fundamental questions. What do we really want in life? Where are we going? What do we want our lives to be five years or ten years from now? If we continue living the way we're living, what will our eternal destination be? Knowing where one is going can greatly help him when it comes to deciding the way he is to follow.

Fourth, "take the way that leads to what is good." Move. Take a stand. No decision is a decision. Joshua said, "I've thought about it. I've considered the possibilities of life, and I've made my decision. For me and my family, we'll serve the Lord God" (see Joshua 24:15). He never regretted that decision.

God has promised to guide us in our lives. He not only knows where we need to go in our lives; he has an excellent way of helping us to get there.

**Trust in the Lord with all your heart. Never rely on what you think you know. Remember the Lord in everything you do, and he will show you the right way. (Prov. 3:5-6, TEV)**

> The really important thing in life is not the avoidance of mistakes, but the obedience of faith. By obedience, the man is led step by step to correct his errors, whereas nothing will ever happen to him if he doesn't get going.[4]

*Lord, I've thought about it. It occurs to me that one reason why some decisions are so hard to make is that I want to be certain I'm doing the right thing. Is that wrong for me to feel that way? Lord, help me to know that you not only "show" the way, you are the way. Help me to follow you as best I can. Through Jesus Christ, I pray. Amen.*

## Creative Tension

What would life be like without tension? I don't know, but sometimes I think I might like to find out. Life is filled with tension of one type or another. All of us are under some kind of pressure.

Yet, when I think of life without tension, I think about that screen door I saw. The power had gone out of the spring that normally held the door firmly shut. Now the door was swaying with the breeze. It was not under control. Maybe life would be as limp as that door without some tension. Maybe that would not be so good.

Muscles develop when they're placed under pressure. The mind expands when it is stretched to receive more information. Individuals have been known to excel when they responded to extraordinary pressure and overcame the obstacles that were against them.

What you and I must do, however, is to determine the source of the tension. Some tension is negative. Some is creative. Negative tension is destructive. Creative tension can help us realize our fullest potential as persons.

Negative tension is produced by several things. Some people are living tension-filled lives in the present because they have never surrendered the past to God's love and forgiveness. Most of us have received some painful experiences in our past. Most of us have done our share of sinning. All of us need to be able to surrender the past to God. We are not strong enough to carry the pressure of its pain. Its door can slam into our faces.

Negative tension is also produced by a wrong set of values. When one tries to prove his worth by the amount of money earned or spent, by the position held, or by the many external signs of human value which we have established, then that one can feel as if he doesn't measure up. Life can become extremely heavy.

On the other hand, creative tension has provided us with individuals whose accomplishments have made life better for all of us. The dreamers, the visionaries, the inventors—all of them lived and worked under tension.

Michelangelo was working under creative tension when he painted biblical history on the ceiling of the Sistine chapel in Rome. Little did he know at the time that future generations would stand in stiff-necked awe as they admired his work of art.

At midnight, George Handel paced the floor. A surging torrent of pent-up emotion kept probing and searching his life, stretching his mind and emotions. Then God spoke in the vernacular of sharps and flats and the great "Hallelujah Chorus" was born. Creative tension emerged the victor.

"Now is my soul troubled [tense—under duress and strain]" (John 12:27), said Christ as he stood in the shadow of the cross. The rest of that story is the drama of redemption.

A religious commitment produces tension. When people try to become individuals whose life-styles resemble Christ's and whose goals are kingdom dreams, they work under pressure. But it's a pressure that produces peace—God's peace. The truth is—we're going to have tension. We simply must choose the kind. One offers nervous breakdowns. The other offers peace.

**Now is my heart troubled—and what shall I say? Shall I say, "Father, do not let this hour come upon me"? But that is why I came—so that I might go through this hour of suffering. Father, bring glory to your name! (John 12:27, TEV)**

> A genuine Christian has an advantage over others since the nature of his faith is akin to crises much like warfare. Born in the tension of a crucifixion, it is part of a dying process that, though waning, is generating new life just as surely as new cells are hourly replacing those which have served their purpose and died off. This person with dual citizenship—one on earth and one in heaven—feels a compulsion from within which the unregenerate can never experience. The Christian interprets this tension as the handwork of God.[5]

*Lord, when I feel the pressure of your hands upon me, help me to remember that the Potter must put pressure on the clay if he is to make a suitable vessel of it. Father, I pray that you will keep me under your divine control and spare me from the tension that is negative and destructive. Amen.*

## The Bitter Pill

Learning to live with the past is one of the greatest challenges we have. The human mind is like a massive storage vault. It absorbs so many details of every experience. Indeed, each moment our eyes are open, they are photographing what they see and developing these pictures in the darkroom of the mind.

The result of this is that we have things in our minds for which we are very thankful—beautiful memories, sweet thoughts of something that was done for us, pleasant recollections of kind words spoken to us or about us. But we also have memories of pain and hurt which we have experienced. Someone may have said something to us that hurt our feelings. We might have been slighted intentionally or unintentionally by someone, and the thought of that mental injury keeps itself fresh in the files of our memories.

Bitterness is a common reaction to the pain of life. To keep from being bitter, some people turn off their thinking. When the thought of some pain is presented to them, they say, "I don't want to talk about it. I don't want to think about it." And they don't. They have a great capacity to forget the injury.

Others are not so blessed. They find themselves thinking about it even when they don't want to think of it. It seems to surface in the most unexpected places. In fact, one could even be enjoying a good relationship or conversation with someone and suddenly, without provocation, some unpleasant memory will sweep through the channels of one's mind. In its wake, it leaves anger, depression, or sadness.

How can we gain the victory in this area of our thinking? How can we receive help? First, let me suggest that we not be guilty of overexpecting from life. Injustices, abuses, and rejection are realities in this world. Some people have been taught to hate and hurt. Others have learned it from their parents and peers. And some have picked it up along the way. Their philosophy is: "Hurt before you get hurt," or "Do unto others before they do unto you."

Second, let me suggest that we not judge the book by its first chapter. The rejection, personal slight, or emotional damage that one receives need not be the final story of that person's life. Some beautiful things have been known to happen in some relationships after shaky beginnings. Through the help of God we can make some good happen in spite of those things that might otherwise create a bitter spirit.

Finally, may I suggest that we release ourselves, our relationships, and the causes of our bitterness to Christ. People who are committed to God still receive their rejection, abuses, and injustices. But because of Christ's spirit, they learn to handle them. Consequently, they live with a greater sense of inner peace.

It serves no good purpose for us to keep reminding ourselves of the pain we have received in the past. It only tends to delay the healing. God can help us overcome the spirit of bitterness. He will give us victory—if we'll allow him that privilege.

**Is there anyone among you who is wise and understanding? He is to prove it by his good life, by his good deeds performed with humility and wisdom. But if in your heart you are jealous, bitter, and selfish, don't sin against the truth by boasting of your wisdom. Such wisdom does not come down from heaven; it belongs to the world, it is unspiritual and demonic. (Jas. 3:13-15, TEV)**

> The really important thing is that in those early days the pagans saw in Christianity and in the Church a power that could cope with and mend the human situation. They saw in Christianity a power which they did not possess—and they wanted it. . . . The greatest converting influence of all is a life which clearly and obviously is possessed of a power which can cope with the human situation in all its problems, in all its tragedy, and in all its pain.[6]

*Lord, I confess to you that it's easy for me to become bitter toward those who seem to delight in hurting others. It's easy to become bitter toward life. There is so much that I don't understand. And Father, since you know my heart, I confess that I've had times of bitterness toward you. I didn't understand you either. Please help me to surrender the causes of my bitterness to the Christ who bore my sins to Calvary. I long for your gentle peace. Amen.*

## The Tea Bag

People demonstrate more about their real character when they are under pressure than when life is moving along rather smoothly. As someone has said, "A good man is like a tea bag; his real strength comes out when he is in hot water." We might also note that his real "flavor" comes out then, too. He adds a bit of refreshment to those who are around him.

We've seen people like that in all areas of life. On the athletic field or the basketball court, he is the person who seems to be unshaken by the mounting pressures of the game. Calmly he goes about his business, and as he does, he gives stability to the other players who might have a tendency to break under the pressure.

In the office, she is the person who seems to be at her best when deadlines are pressing. Without raising her voice, without complaining about the amount of work that must be done, she simply does the task at hand. Her serenity gives quiet dignity to others who work with her.

In the home, perhaps it is the mother who says, "Now let's just settle down and talk about this—one at a time, please. Keep your voices soft. Don't get excited. We're going to work our way through this problem."

The world is a better place in which to live because of the people who are able to take the pressure without exploding. All of us know the tensions of life. All of us experience them. Even an infant feels some pressure. Our circumstances are not made better by people who scream and throw things. They're not helped by those who shout obscenities and criticisms. If our situations are to be made better, indeed, if the world is to be made better, there must be more people whose real strength comes out when they are in "hot water."

Jesus is a good example for us to follow. The pressure was on. Everyone was uptight. The air was heavy with mounting hostility toward Christ. Judas had already been approached about the possibility of collaborating with the enemy to deliver Jesus into their hands. James and John had already asked if they could have the best positions when Jesus got into power. The other disciples resented such high-handed self-promotion.

They sat at the table eating the Passover meal. It was quiet—not a reverent quietness that one might have expected, but a sulking, pouting quietness. Then Jesus "rose from the table, took off his outer garment, and tied a towel around his waist" (John 13:4, TEV). With great calmness and magnificent inner strength he began to wash the disciples' feet and dry them with the towel. Everyone felt the power of his composure.

The "hot water" is certain to come to all of us as we make our journeys through life. We can be burned up by it, or, like Christ, we can "flavor" the situation.

**You, Lord, give perfect peace**
**to those who keep their purpose firm**
**and put their trust in you. (Isa. 26:3, TEV)**

> People then should rejoice in suffering, strange as it sounds, for this is a sign of the availability of energy to transform their characters. Suffering is nature's method of indicating a mistaken attitude or way of behavior, and to the . . . non-egocentric person every moment of suffering is the opportunity for growth.[7]

*Lord, in these troubled times filled with pressures and distractions, help me to have the inner peace that only you can give. Keep me calm amidst the conflict. Let me be an example of the strength you give to your children. Through Jesus Christ, our Lord. Amen.*

## "Help Me to Be Good, But . . . "

I heard about a young woman who prayed, "Lord, help me to be good, but don't fence me in." We have another way of saying the same thing. We talk about people "who want to have their cake and eat it, too." I suppose there's something in all of us that would lead us to want the prize without the price, the victory without the struggle, the pat on the head without the work of the hands.

"Help me to be good . . . " I would really like to be able to have a clean and clear conscience, that inner feeling of peace that all is well with myself as I make my way through this life.

"Help me to be good . . . " I want to do the right things, those things that will make the world a better place in which all of us can experience goodness, kindness, and peace.

"But don't fence me in." That too is a part of our real feelings. We don't like restrictions. Ideally, I suppose that we'd like to be able to set the guidelines and rules about what is considered to be "good." Sometimes it seems to make no difference to us that the Lord God said to that couple in primeval times, "All the fruit of the garden you may eat, but don't touch the tree in the center of the garden" (see Gen. 2:16-17). All of the trees versus one. Yet, when the statement is made that way, it is the "one" that is so dreadfully tempting. "Don't fence me in." Had God said nothing about the "one tree" that tree would not have been nearly so interesting.

Perhaps another factor that made the temptation so tempting was the location of the tree. It was planted right in the center of the garden, right in the main intersection. Had it been located on some side street far removed from the beaten path, Adam and Eve may not have had much difficulty with it. But it was so available. It was there every day.

That's why some of our temptations are as tempting as they are. They are available to us. Of course, they're off limits to us, and that causes us to do some extra thinking. We wonder what it would be like if we ate the fruit of the tree. "Lord, help me to be good, but don't fence me in."

How can we learn to be good while being "fenced in"? There are two very helpful suggestions. First, we must learn to be absolutely honest with ourselves and our weaknesses. The person is a fool who tries to alibi to himself and thus deceive himself. Be honest with yourself. Accept God's kind word of instruction. He knows what is good for us and what is evil. There are some things in life that will do us harm. God "fences" us in. He tries to protect us.

Second, we must have outside help. We don't have the strength to overcome temptations. We need God's strength. He can enable us to be good. He can even help us to enjoy the "fence." Let us surrender ourselves and our temptations to him. We'll be glad we did.

**For it is clear that it is not the angels that he helps. Instead, as the scripture says, "He helps the descendants of Abraham." This means that he had to become like his brothers in every way, in order to be their faithful and merciful High Priest in his service to God, so that the people's sins would be forgiven. And now he can help those who are tempted, because he himself was tempted and suffered. (Heb. 2:16-18, TEV)**

> I resolve to meet evil courageously, but when even a small temptation cometh, I am in sore straits. That which seemeth trifling sometimes giveth rise to a grievous temptation; and when I think myself to be secure, and least expect it, I am overcome by a light breath.[8]

*Dear Heavenly Father, thank you for the fences. Help me to know that you did not build them to keep me in, but to keep evil and its subsequent suffering out. Just as I try to protect my children from that which would harm them, I thank you for loving me enough to want to protect me, too. Help me to trust your love. Amen.*

## "Hang in There, Baby"

It was New Year's Day at Pete's house. His grandfather, a man fully ninety-four years of age, was there, and so were many of the old gentleman's sons and daughters, grandsons and granddaughters, even great-grandsons and great-granddaughters. It was quite a crowd.

The bowl games were on television. Children were playing with their Christmas toys. The ladies were trying to rest from their meal preparation and housecleaning, and the men were wandering from the television to the scraps of turkey and boxes of chocolates. Perhaps it was just a typical after-Christmas, first of the year, family reunion.

The grandfather's heart was weak, and so he wore a pacemaker, a small, battery-operated device, that has helped prolong the life of many people. Halftime had come to the football game, and the old gentleman was left alone in front of the television.

That's where our story begins. The band was performing on the football field, and the lovely majorettes were tossing their batons into the air. Pete happened to be standing behind his grandfather, his presence undetected. When the cameraman provided a close-up shot of one of the beautiful girls, Pete said, "Granddad was sitting on the edge of his chair tapping his pacemaker and saying, 'Don't go out now! Don't go out now!'"

Had the man been thirty-four, that would not have been such big news. But at the age of ninety-four, he was fully alert and alive and indicating his appreciation of an attractive girl.

For him life was still worth living. He could make people laugh. He could enjoy a good laugh on himself. He hadn't given up on himself even though his age and health conditions were against him. "Life," for him, "had not lost its lovely look."

There is something splendid about a person who has lived long and well and has retained his or her capacity to be an enjoyable person. One's attitude toward life makes so much difference. Ninety-four years is a long time. The man's life began in another century. It spanned from the days of the horse and buggy to the space age. He had seen two major world wars and several minor ones. He knew the distress of the Depression. Yet, through it all, he maintained a strong faith in God and believed in God's power to help and heal the brokenness of life.

God enabled the old gentleman to appreciate the good qualities in people. He helped him overlook the faults and failures that time and circumstances will give us all. At age ninety-four, he was "hanging in there." He had given no thought to the idea of quitting.

It is God who can enable us to think like that and live like that. It is faith in God which can help us to go on when quitting would be easier. It is the blessed gift which the Creator gives that helps us to enjoy the present and anticipate the future. What God has done for others, he can do for you. Hang in there! Trust him. He wants to help you—right now!

**I look to the mountains;**
**where will my help come from?**
**My help will come from the Lord,**
**who made heaven and earth.**

**He will not let you fall;**
**your protector is always awake.**
**(Ps. 121:1-3, TEV)**

> Life is a movement, evolution, progression and not stagnation; it can be comprehended only in its incessant becoming, in its total continuity. You need a sense of history if you are to make sense of life. If you look only at the point where you are, you will see neither where you came from nor where you are going. One of the dimensions of your consciousness as a living being is missing if you do not enter into relationship with all age-groups, and more particularly with those who are nearing the end of their lives.[9]

*Lord, I thank you for all the people I know who have reached the sunset years of their lives. I see in them a quiet confidence, and I am encouraged. I know they've had some of the same struggles that I experience, and yet you have enabled them to overcome. That thought strengthens me. Lord, help me to hang in there, too. In Jesus' name, I pray. Amen.*

# Looking for Miracles

"Boy, it would take a miracle for us to win now," he said as he bleakly watched his losing team. "Nothing short of a miracle could save the life of your husband," the doctor told the woman whose face showed the strain of fear and whose eyes were moist from her crying.

In his book *Bread For The Wilderness, Wine For The Journey,* John Killinger describes his journey from doubt to faith.

> How to see again! That is what we want. How to live every day as though the world were paradise and not wilderness, as though all of life were filled with the miracles of God!
>
> That is what we desire more than anything else—to see miracles again![10]

People have always looked for miracles. Ours is a world of limitations. Time and space block us in. Our strength is limited. Some human situations are like walls and bars that hold us prisoner. "Impossible," we say, "this circumstance is impossible. My world will never be any better than it is right now. I have no hope."

I suppose people have historically looked at life in much the same way. This leads to that, and that leads to this. It's all so automatic. Cause and effect. "Sow a thought, and you reap an act:/Sow an act, and you reap a habit;/Sow a habit, and you reap a character;/Sow a character, and you reap a destiny." There is no stopping the wheels once they get rolling. There are no miracles in life.

But that's just the point. There are miracles! A miracle is an interruption of the routine. It is a reversal of that which seems irreversible. In some ways, it is an interruption of an unalterable law. But miracles do happen. We talk about our "miracle wins" in athletics. We call some recoveries of health the result of a miracle.

Our world is not so automatic that everything is what it is and will be what it will be. There is God. There is prayer. There is hope, for there are miracles.

In some cases, the miracle changes the circumstance. Of course, that's what we pray for. That's what we hope for. We want our circumstances and situations to be changed. We want people to be changed. We want history to be changed. And sometimes we get what we want. It may not happen all at once, but it happens. God meets us and presents miracles to us.

In other cases, the miracle changes the person. The circumstance remains the same, but the individual is enabled to cope with it, to handle it, to live a beautiful life in spite of the adversity. That too is a miracle.

"Life can be a wilderness or a paradise," said Killinger. "It's the point of view—of how you see things." God has the power to change your circumstance or your viewpoint. In either case, that's a miracle! Are you ready for a miracle? Are you ready for God to make a miracle—of you?

**"I do not know if he is a sinner or not," the man replied. "One thing I do know: I was blind, and now I see." (John 9:25, TEV)**

> The evidence of lives changed by contact with Christ is so abundant that the full story can never be told; it is, indeed, of a kind not matched anywhere in any culture. The changed lives have come about, not primarily by a set of ideas or by acceptance of a doctrine, but by commitment to a Person.[11]

*Lord, I thank you that you have given us enough miracles in our past for us to anticipate a few more in our present. Just as you parted the waters to deliver the Hebrew children, part the waters of doubt so that I too might walk through on dry land. Roll away a few stones. Open a few eyes. Help us to look for salvation—the greatest miracle of them all. Amen.*

# 4
# CARE

Who cares? I care. Who needs care? You need care. I need care. All of us need care. But what is care? Is it just a sweet-sounding word? The billboard said: TO CARE IS TO SHARE. Is that true? Suppose you can't cure; should you still try to care? Is it right to "cure" without "caring"? Care does not mean that one can always cure, does it? It may not mean that one can cure at all. Perhaps it means, "I'll walk with you. I'll listen to you. I'll share your burden. I'll stand by you." God cares. He cares about the hairs on one's head and the sparrows that fall. He cares about you and me. God's best to us is care—real care, Calvary care. He cares!

## Who Cares Anyway?

One day a man saw a small boy who wanted to go outdoors to play with some older children, but he was afraid they wouldn't accept him. When the children began to return to the house, the man suggested to the lad, "Let's hide behind the curtain, and they won't know where we are." The boy looked at him rather sadly and said, "Suppose they don't care?"

"Suppose they don't care?" Suppose it won't matter to them where we are. Suppose they won't even bother to look. Suppose we hid behind the curtain until the end of the day, until the end of time, and no one ever bothered to come to look for us?

For many people, that's where their pain is. They are not being mistreated by others. No one is smacking their faces. No one hurls bricks at them. No one beats them with sticks. No one cares enough to do that. They simply are ignored. They're treated as if they were part of the wallpaper. Some people feel they're nothing more than department store mannequins—to be walked around but not related to.

Have you ever had someone talking to you and looking past you at the same time? There are people who seem to be always on the "prowl" for someone more important. Even while they're passing some time talking with you, they're looking for someone else who might be more important to them.

Perhaps you were standing with another person when someone approached. Your friend got the excited greetings. You received a halfhearted nod of the head. Your friend received the compliments and care while you looked and listened.

"Suppose they don't care." Many people live their entire lives with treatment like that. They don't seek it. They don't want it. They don't feel comfortable with it, but they don't know what to do about it.

They may not, but we do. We who are the speakers, we who are the complimenters, we who are the greeters. We can do something about it.

For one thing, we can be sensitive to the needs of each individual and not to the select few who are beautiful, powerful, or important. We can be aware of the "other" person who is there. We can take time. We can say, "Why don't you join us?"

Jesus was great at "seeing" the little people. One day he stopped a processional to help a woman who had had a disease for 12 years—a woman who had given up on life. Another day he saw a rejected man and said, "Come down from the tree; I'd like to eat dinner with you this evening" (Luke 19:5, author's paraphrase). He saw an adulteress whom others wanted to stone. He wanted to give her a second chance.

The world is grossly overpopulated with people who don't care. It needs a few more like Jesus. Who cares anyway?

**You will be doing the right thing if you obey the law of the Kingdom, which is found in the scripture, "Love your neighbor as you love yourself." But if you treat people according to their outward appearance, you are guilty of sin, and the Law condemns you as a lawbreaker. (Jas. 2:8-9, TEV)**

> To love is to will the good for another. Love may mean writing with enough care so that our correspondent can read without spending time deciphering; that is, it may mean taking the time to save his time. To love is to pay one's bills; it is to keep things in order so that the wife's work will be made easier. It means arriving somewhere on time; it means giving your full attention to the one who is talking to you. To miss what he says means that we are more interested in what we are telling ourselves inwardly than in what he is telling us. To love is to try to speak in his language, even if we have mastered it but poorly, rather than to force him to speak ours.[1]

*Lord, I pray as the guilty one. I confess that there are times when I abuse the feelings and needs of others. Help me to care enough to give my very best of time, attention, and kindness to those who wonder if anybody cares. Teach me how to* really care. *Through Christ, I pray. Amen.*

## Please Look at Me

In one of the touching scenes in Thornton Wilder's *Our Town,* Emily is allowed to come back from the dead to Grover's Corners to relive her twelfth birthday. Her mother was so excited about it. She wanted to make it a very special time. There she stood in her kitchen preparing for the occasion while Emily was trying to talk with her. Finally, out of frustration, Emily cried out, "Oh, Mama, just look at me for one minute as though you really saw me."

All of us are busy. The children are. The youth are. The adults are. Everyone is. In fact, we just might be too busy.

Several years ago a teenage girl from one of our Southern cities was talking with a teenage girl who lived in a small mountain town in southeastern Kentucky. The city girl was quite bewildered that in the mountain community where she was visiting there were no tennis courts, no community swimming pool, no bowling alleys, and no theaters. "What do you do for fun?" she asked.

The pretty mountain girl smiled warmly and said, "Those of you who live in cities that have all of those things find that you have to turn to them to make you happy and give you something to do. If one doesn't have 'things' to turn to, one turns to people. That's what we do. I guess our fun is in being with each other. We develop deep friendships."

Needless to say, it was a good answer—an answer that my city friend could not identify with, however, because her life was filled with things to do and places to go.

If we are to develop the kind of friendships in our families and among our associates that will be fulfilling to us, we must take the time to look at them and stop doing those things which we think we just have to do.

Surely Emily would have been happy to have a big birthday cake. Who wouldn't? But more than the cake, she wanted her mother's undivided attention. She wanted her mother's time. "Please look at me."

Jesus knew how to do that. He made people feel pretty important. He gave them dignity and respect. It didn't matter what had to be done, where he was going, what time it was. He took time for the individual. He took time for the children. We remember people who do that, don't we? We love them for it.

By the way, is there anyone today who could really benefit from a few minutes of your time? Is there a husband or wife, a son or daughter, a parent or friend who would like to have some of your undivided attention? Is there someone who seems to be crying out to you, "Please look at me one minute as though you really saw me"? Perhaps it's time we started looking.

**She had a sister named Mary, who sat down at the feet of the Lord and listened to his teaching. Martha was upset over all the work she had to do, so she came and said, "Lord, don't you care that my sister has left me to do all the work by myself? Tell her to come and help me!"**

**The Lord answered her, "Martha, Martha! You are worried and troubled over so many things, but just one is needed. Mary has chosen the right thing, and it will not be taken away from her." (Luke 10:39-42, TEV)**

> To love is to give one's time. We never give the impression that we care when we are in a hurry. . . . I am ever struck by the tranquility in which Christ walked along, always having time to speak with a poor woman beside a well, or replying to the stupid questions of his disciples the very eve of his Passion. To exercise a spiritual ministry means to take time.[2]

*Thank you, Jesus, that you took the time to stop and talk with so many people. Thank you, Jesus, that you took the time to give me your undivided attention, your undivided love. Help me to stop, look, and listen to those who are crying for help. Amen.*

## Compliments

The man said, "I heard a compliment about you the other day. Later on I want to share it with you." And "later on" seemed never to come. It seemed like an eternity from the moment he said he had heard the compliment to the time when he shared it. Why did it seem so long? Because a compliment is a cherished gift; because all of us want to be loved and appreciated; because we have a great hunger for an expression of praise.

Everyone enjoys hearing kind words. No matter how young we are or how old we become, there is still something good about the appreciation we can receive from the words of others. There is an inner satisfaction derived in knowing that someone approves of our appearance, our work, or our contribution to life. All of us need affirming words.

But not all of us get them. Some of us live in the shadows of those who do better what we do best. We don't excel at anything. We're extremely common. When compared to others we're not as pretty, not as smart, not as talented, not as well dressed, and not as successful. Yet we have a hunger for praise, a strong need for love and appreciation. In fact, people who don't excel probably need compliments more than people who do excel.

Compliments are ways of saying, "I care about you. I appreciate you. I approve of you." All of us need care, appreciation, and approval.

Maybe the Golden Rule can help us at this point. "Do unto others as you would have others do unto you." If we enjoy being appreciated by others, perhaps we should learn to show appreciation for others. If words can lift our spirits, we should learn to use them in a manner whereby we can lift the spirits of others.

"I like to give my roses to the living," the woman said. Then she told the other person of her appreciation of the contribution that she had made to her life. And why not? If people can be blessed by our compliments, why not bless them?

I really don't know how Jesus used compliments, but I know he must have used them frequently and well. He had the uncanny ability to make people feel good about themselves. He knew how to lift their spirits. They enjoyed his company. Christ has given us an example that we should follow in his steps—even in our complimenting.

Think about it. Is there someone right now who needs to be told of some great contribution he or she is making to your life? Is there a pencil or pen handy? How about the telephone? Compliments are wonderful to receive. They're nice to give, too.

**I remember your tears, and I want to see you very much, so that I may be filled with joy. I remember the sincere faith you have, the kind of faith that your grandmother Lois and your mother Eunice also had. I am sure that you have it also. (2 Tim. 1:4-5, TEV)**

> When Jesus gave Simon a new self-concept symbolized by the name Peter—a rock—He set in motion this divine inner mechanism. God was now at work in Simon, helping him to become Simon Peter, Simon the Rock of towering strength.[3]

*Father in heaven, I thank you for the wonderful compliment you gave us when you showed your love through Christ. Our lives have light because of his light. His belief in us enables us to believe in ourselves. Lord, as you have given so much to us, help us to find ways of giving hope, help, and encouragement to others. Enable us to recognize the beauty in others, and Lord, don't let us forget to tell them. Amen.*

## Somebody's Wallace

Many beautiful stories have come down to us from the days of Abraham Lincoln. One related the incident of two women, relatives of General Lew Wallace, who sought news at the White House concerning his situation. After learning he had survived a vicious battle, they spoke rather glibly of their gladness that the one casualty named "Wallace" was not "our Wallace." To which

Lincoln responded, "Yes, but it was somebody's Wallace, wasn't it?"

Sometimes when we receive good news about ourselves and about those whom we love, we are so relieved that we tend to forget the pain and heartache of those who were not, and are not, as blessed as we. I hope it isn't that we are so hardened or selfish as to not really care about the predicament of others. I think it's just that we are so elated about our own circumstances that we tend to forget others might be suffering some sort of pain.

"It was somebody's Wallace, wasn't it?" Yes. So that means that others are going to be hurt and grief stricken when they discover their "Wallace" didn't survive the battle. Do we care?

There is a great deal of hurting that goes on around us daily—among some of the people we know quite well and some of those we do not. Some live in close proximity to us. Some do not. Some we might feel helpless to help. Some we might not care to help. Some we do not know how to help.

I remember two statements Jesus made, and he made them in close connection with each other. When a group of Greek citizens sought him not long before his crucifixion, he said, "Now is my soul troubled" (John 12:27). Shortly thereafter he said to his disciples, "Let not your heart be troubled" (John 14:1). "My troubles . . . your troubles." In the midst of his troubled soul, he was concerned about their troubled souls.

Can we be that sensitive, that caring, that concerned? Can we learn how to be glad that "our Wallace" survived, yet equally as grieved that "somebody's Wallace" did not make it? If we can, then we are able to say that we have the spirit of Jesus. "I am troubled," he said in effect, "but I am concerned about your trouble."

Jesus showed us what compassion really means. He got "outside" himself and into the lives of people. He literally spent himself for others. His eyes were busy eyes, searching eyes, piercing eyes. He saw what others did not see, what others were conditioned not to see. He saw the pain inside of people and, like a master sculptor, he hammered and chiseled until he dug it out.

It's OK to be glad that "our Wallace" made it through the battle. But let us not forget that "somebody's Wallace" didn't. Like Christ, we must learn how to care for the hurting and help them where we can.

**Be happy with those who are happy, weep with those who weep. Have the same concern for everyone. (Rom. 12:15-16*a*, TEV)**

She rushed to my arms
With eight-year-old candor
Broken heart
Tears
*Mary didn't pass—*
*We won't be together next year.*
Fourth grade tragedy.
Separated friends . . .
Here in our town
There are countless Marys
Countless Joes
Who may never pass
From death unto life.
Eternal tragedy
Separated families
Lord
Does my heart break?
Have I shed a single tear?[4]

*Heavenly Father, I thank you for all the blessings that have come to me. I pray for all of those whose lives are not as blessed. Don't allow me the ecstasy of celebrating "our Wallace" without having the compassion for the "Wallaces" who don't make it. Help me to really care. Amen.*

## Get Lost!

"Get lost!" That's what the girls said to a younger brother who seemed to always show up when they were ready to have a tea party for their dolls. That's also what a lot of older "children" say to those who are doing things that make them a nuisance. "Get lost! Get out of my way! Get out of my life!"

Some of us need to "get lost"—but in a different way than that which the term normally means. We need to lose ourselves in something bigger than ourselves. As someone once said, "The trick is to get your mind off yourself, and yourself off your mind."

During World War II, a young woman suffered the loss of her physician husband while they were working in India. Her sadness and grief were so great that living or dying were one and the same to her. She could not conceive of life without him.

Enroute back to the United States aboard a ship, she was approached by a little seven-year-old boy whose missionary parents had been killed in Burma. "You and I," he said, "are the only Americans on this ship." Somehow in his own childish way he thought that was reason enough for them to be special friends to one another. She, however, wanted no special friends. She just wanted him and everyone else to "get lost."

During the night, the ship on which they were passengers was torpedoed and began to sink. Her first impulse was to go down with the vessel. About that time she saw the little boy shivering in fear like a terrified animal. "He came to me," she later said, "and clung close. He needed me."

For several days they were adrift in the South Atlantic, and finally they were rescued. They managed to pull one another through. Later, the lady's friends said it would be difficult to say who had saved whom: whether it was the woman who had saved the child, or the child who had saved the woman.

Some of us are literally losing our lives while trying to save them. Life was meant to be spent. It was meant to be shared. Jesus said, "Greater love hath no man than this, that a man lay down his life for his friends. Ye are my friends" (John 15:13-14*a*). He also said, "Whoever would save his life will lose it; and whoever loses his life for my sake, he will save it" (Luke 9:24, RSV).

Peace of mind does not come from self-centeredness and self-saving. If we are to experience the joy of a quiet mind, we must learn the art of self-giving.

Someone has said,

> Seldom can the heart be lonely,
> If it seeks a lonelier still;
> Self-forgetting, seeking only
> Emptier cups of love to fill.

Life is filled with pleasant surprises for the person who learns to "get lost" in meeting the needs of others. The choice is ours—We can either get "in" the way and become a hindrance, or we can get "on" the way toward becoming a helper. Do you care?

**I am telling you the truth: a grain of wheat remains no more than a single grain unless it is dropped into the ground and dies. If it does die, then it produces many grains. (John 12:24, TEV)**

> Love is not just some great abstract idea or feeling. There are some people with such a lofty conception of love that they never succeed in expressing it in the simple kindnesses of ordinary life. They dream of heroic devotion and self-sacrifice. But, waiting for the opportunity that never comes, they make themselves very unlikeable to those near them and never sense their neighbors' need for affection.[5]

*Lord, I thank you that in Jesus Christ you have given to us a perfect example of what it means to "get lost" in the service of others. He lost his life in the process, but you rewarded him with a resurrection. Help me to learn the art of "getting lost" in love and service to others. Through Christ, I pray. Amen.*

## Mirrors

"Who do you think you are?" Has anyone ever asked you that question? Usually, it's a criticism—a put-down, a way of questioning our right to do something.

May I ask it in a slightly different manner—"Who do you *think* you are?" In a way, it makes very little difference who you are. What one *thinks* about oneself is what matters.

Fortunately, or unfortunately, whichever the case may be for us, we draw much of our feelings or thoughts about ourselves from the "mirrors" we look into. Some of those mirrors are silver painted. They reveal our physical appearance to us. We may not like what we see, but over a period of time, we either improve our physical appearances through cosmetics, hair styles, clothing, and the like, or we just become accustomed to that face in the mirror.

Perhaps more importantly than the glass mirrors are the flesh and blood type called "people." We're either OK or not OK in our way of thinking because of the approval or disapproval we receive from people. If they compliment and encourage us, we tend to develop good thoughts about ourselves. If they criticize and reject us, we tend to develop poor self-images.

But think about this. Have you ever looked at yourself in a "curved" mirror? Maybe it was one of those crazy mirrors one might see at a carnival, or perhaps it could even be your reflection on the chrome surface of a car bumper. Anyway, you probably laughed at the distortion you saw. You knew it wasn't an accurate resemblance of the "real" you. Well, suppose some people are like those "curved" mirrors. The problem is not in the one who looks into the "mirror"—it's the "mirror" that has the problem.

You and I should not allow the opinions of other people to become so heavy to us that we think of ourselves the way they think. They may be the ones who are having the "image" problems. Not all people are good "mirrors."

I'm glad that one day I found a perfect "mirror." His name is Jesus. When I looked at him, I saw myself not only as I was, but as I could become. He forgave my sins and washed my face. He looked at me and said, "Jerry, you're worth something. You're valuable to me. You're unique." My self-esteem improved drastically.

It's nice to have the approval of people. We need some of that, too. But let me suggest this to you. Let Christ be your "mirror." Draw your opinion of yourself from his love and acceptance of you. "Groom" yourself according to his way of living and loving. If you do, I'll guarantee this. First, you'll feel good and think well of yourself, and second, you'll receive a good measure of approval and affirmation from others.

**Then he took Simon to Jesus.**

**Jesus looked at him and said, "Your name is Simon son of John, but you will be called Cephas." (This is the same as Peter and means "a rock.") (John 1:42, TEV)**

> Sometimes at that moment [in despair] a wave of light breaks into our darkness, and it is as though a voice were saying: "You are accepted. *You are accepted,* accepted by that which is greater than you."[6]

*Father, there is nothing that can make a person feel better than the sweet feeling of being loved, wanted, cared for, and accepted. That's what you did for me in Jesus Christ. That's what you continue to do for me day by day as I read your word. I am encouraged by your forgiveness and acceptance. Thank you for wanting me. Amen.*

## Words

When I was growing up, I remember someone saying to me: "Sticks and stones may break my bones,/But words will never hurt me."

I have lived long enough to know how terribly wrong that statement is. Words have so much power latent within them. They have started wars. They have led to divorces. The irresponsible use of words has led more than one person down the road to heartbreak. Some people spend all of their time trying to recover a good self-image that the words of others has destroyed.

"Sticks may break my bones." Indeed they might. Weapons of force do extensive damage to our bodies. But words can break our spirits. They can stymie our initiative. They can inhibit our willpower. They have even been known to take away one's will to live.

People who make it a practice to cut down and criticize the life and work of others should have a deeper understanding of the power of words. We should be aware of the fact that if our words have the power to destroy, they also have the power to build. Affirming words, loving words, words that lift have often "saved" lives.

Then there are others who seem to have the uncanny ability to say what they don't mean. We sometimes say that this is the "foot-in-mouth" disease.

So often people say things to others that are received differently than the speaker intended. Consequently, the good that might have been done actually became a negative message. And that can be bad, too.

I don't know if there is a permanent cure for such an illness except to say that it might be better for us to put our brains in gear before putting our mouths in motion. We won't always say what we should, but perhaps we can do a better job with our expressions.

Jesus told us that we would be judged by our idle words. Anything that is "idle" is unproductive. Nothing good is produced. Perhaps our Lord was trying to tell us that our words should build and not destroy. Maybe he was trying to remind us that God has good ears. He hears our words.

Anyway, I know some people who are just dying to hear some good words about themselves. So, "Let the words of my mouth, and the meditation of my heart, be acceptable in thy sight, O Lord, my strength, and my redeemer" (Ps. 19:14). Let them also be acceptable to people who need them.

**But no one has ever been able to tame the tongue. It is evil and uncontrollable, full of deadly poison. We use it to give thanks to our Lord and Father and also to curse our fellow-man, who is created in the likeness of God. Words of thanksgiving and cursing pour forth out from the same mouth. My brothers, this should not happen! (Jas. 3:8-10, TEV)**

> By words one of us can give to another the greatest happiness or bring about utter despair . . . Words call forth emotions and are universally the means by which we influence our fellow creatures.[7]

*Lord, I know about the power of words. My spirit has been lifted to the gates of heaven when someone has used the right words. And my spirit has known the depths of despair when someone has been careless with words. Thank you, Lord, for your words of love, forgiveness, hope, help, and care. Help me to learn your vocabulary. Amen.*

## What Do You Say to a Drowning Man?

What do you say to a drowning man? How about this? "Hey fellow, what's the matter? Can't you swim? Maybe the next time you'll stay out of the deep water."

What do you say to a homemaker who has just burned the evening meal? How about this? "You stupid woman! Can't you see that the meat loaf was left in the oven about ten minutes too long?"

What do you say to a ten-year-old boy who has just struck out with the winning run standing on third base? How about this? "Kid, what in the world were you thinking about? Don't you know that a hit would have won the game for us?"

What do you say to someone who has just failed at anything? Of course, we wouldn't say that to a drowning man, or a disappointed cook, or a brokenhearted little boy. People aren't that cruel. Or, are they?

Some parents have a difficult time commending their children for the good the children are doing, but they're quite eloquent when it comes to chastising them for their failures.

Some companions easily spot the negative characteristics in their mate's behavior, but they're nearly blind when it comes to appreciation of the good character traits.

Some employers are sharp in their criticism of an employee when a product is not manufactured, boxed, or marketed as well as it might have been. Those same employers are not as quick to praise the same people for jobs well done.

People who fail usually don't need to be reminded they have failed. If one fails and cannot see the failure, then some word might be necessary. But most people know when they haven't succeeded. They're not pleased with the failure any more than their critics are. Continuing to criticize a person when he is down is no way to respond to a "drowning man."

There was a time in the life of Christ when his friends failed. They were physically tired. They had been deprived of sleep because of a rigorous, whirlwind schedule. They were under severe mental pressure.

Jesus said, "Watch and pray with me for one hour." They didn't. They went to sleep. "What do you say to a drowning man?" What did Jesus say? "Rise, let *us* be going." It was another way of saying, "This time you failed, but I believe in you. I care for you. I forgive you. There's more to come; so let's get on our way."

Is it any wonder that those same people were willing to die for him later on? People are fond of people who give them a second chance. People appreciate people who refuse to treat them as failures—even when they have failed. So, what do *you* say to a drowning man?

**The teachers of the Law and the Pharisees brought in a woman who had been caught committing adultery, and they made her stand before them all. "Teacher," they said to Jesus, "this woman was caught in the very act of committing adultery. In our Law Moses commanded that such a woman must be stoned to death. Now, what do you say?" . . . he straightened up and said to them, "Whichever one of you has committed no sin may throw the first stone at her." (John 8:3-5,7*b*, TEV)**

> There are many religions which know no divine welcome to the sinner until he has ceased to be one. They would first make him righteous, and then bid him welcome to God. But God in Christ first welcomes him penitent and redeems him.[8]

*Lord, I thank you that your love for me is not dependent upon my successes. And I pray that the way you respond to my failures will be the way I learn to respond to the failures of others. Maybe both of us—I and they—can learn to succeed as we respond to forgiving love. Amen.*

## O Say, Can You See?

How well can you see? When I was in the third grade I decided that I wanted to wear glasses. I didn't need them, but I had a friend who wore them. I thought he really looked neat. He was popular. He was a good athlete. He was smart. He just had everything together, and when he put on his glasses, well, that gave him a sophisticated dignity to me.

I told my parents of my need to wear glasses. I'm not certain they really believed my tale of woe, but nevertheless, I was taken to the optometrist. As I recall, the mistake I made in the vision test was to say I couldn't see those four or five big letters on the third line. I remember the expression on the doctor's face. He acted like he didn't believe me. I knew I had messed up my chances of wearing glasses—at least as a third grader. My problem was more in my head—ego gratification. I had no problem with my eyes.

I know a lot of people who have "eye" problems. You can also spell that with the letter "I." Ego problems. Some of us would do almost anything to be more important to ourselves and others. We have an "I" problem.

Our "I" problem often causes us to have "eye" problems, too. That is, we're so wrapped up in ourselves that we can't see beyond ourselves. The priest and Levite had an "I" problem. They were important people. The sacred services at the Temple depended upon their leadership. Indeed, they were so tied up in themselves that they never saw the beaten and bleeding man beside the road. (See Luke 10:20-37.) But some of us are just as guilty.

Jesus once told his disciples, "Lift up your eyes" (John 4:35). People talk about having a "face-lift." But what about an "eye-lift"? We need to get our eyes off ourselves and our circumstances and begin to see others and their needs.

O say, can you see? Can you see what a child might become? Can you see a fine man or woman in that struggling teenager? Can you see the flower in the rosebud? William Blake said it this way:

> To see a world in a grain of sand
> And a heaven in a wild flower,
> Hold infinity in the palm of your hand
> And eternity in an hour.[9]

Some people can see the potential in the lump of clay—the potential of some useful vessel or work of art. Others see only the energy, time, and discipline necessary to make it into something beautiful. There's a world of difference between the two. The people who "see" are the ones who bless life. The others extract blessings.

Jesus had good eyesight. He saw the despairing look on a blind beggar's face. He saw a banquet in a lad's lunch. He saw a million dollars in a widow's mite. He saw God's kingdom get its start in a motley crew of fishermen and small-town businessmen. And one day, he saw me. He loved me, died for me, and day by day he leads me to become the person he knows I can become—a child of God. And that's good eyesight!

**But the Lord said to him, "Pay no attention to how tall and handsome he is. I have rejected him, because I do not judge as man judges. Man looks at the outward appearance, but I look at the heart." (1 Sam. 16:7, TEV)**

> When we treat man as he is, we make him worse than he is. When we treat him as if he already were what he potentially could be, we make him what he should be.[10]

*What a wonderful day it was, O God, when you saw me as a nine-year-old boy. You touched my life that October night and anointed my head and heart with your precious Spirit. Since that time, you have seen far more in me than I have ever been able to see in myself. Thank you for your confidence. Maybe some day I'll see what you see. Lord, help me to trade my "I" problem to receive your "eye" solution. Amen.*

## Being Sought

A man who was rescued from his raft after many days of being adrift on the ocean was asked, "What gave you courage?" He answered, "Knowing that I was being sought."

"Knowing that I was being sought . . . " Knowing that someone else cared about him. Knowing that even as he tried to find his way home that someone was working on the other end of the line trying to reach him. Knowing that the planes would be circling overhead, the boats would be out in force, and the instruments of science would be employed to their fullest capacity as people tried to find a man. He also knew that cost was not a factor. People have been known to spend thousands of dollars on manpower and equipment as they have searched for lost children and lost adults.

"Knowing that I was being sought . . . " That gave the man the courage he needed. Do you know why? Because he knew that if he were being sought, there was hope. You and I won't go far in life without hope. We've got to have it. We've got to feel that there is light at the end of the tunnel—a way out of the abyss. Even people with diseases that presently seem incurable live with hope—hope that medical science will find a breakthrough—hope that God will perform a miracle in their bodies. We've got to have hope, and hope comes from knowing that someone cares, that someone is seeking us.

Francis Thompson wrote that moving poetic drama about the "hound of heaven." It's the story of one man's life—a life spent running from God.

> I fled Him, down the nights and down the days;
> I fled Him, down the arches of the years;
> I fled Him, down the labyrinthine ways

Of my own mind; and in the mist of tears
I hid from Him.[11]

But God was like "the hound of heaven" who relentlessly pursued the runner until at last he found him. And that's our real hope—that no matter how far we may run—no matter what choices we may make in life—no matter how deeply entrenched we might become in our selfishness and sin—God is still on the trail, looking, searching, and caring about us. There's joy in knowing we're "being sought."

We must caution ourselves, however, from thinking that it will ultimately lead to the rescue. It doesn't always happen that way. Men floating at sea on life rafts are not always found. The sea is so vast. A raft is so small. Human visibility is so limited.

Likewise, we must not presume upon God's love. Our God will not overwhelm us into submission. He will not take us against our will. He pursues us with the love of Christ and others, but sooner or later, those who are "being sought" must want to "be found." When that happens, once more there is a "rescue at sea." And there is joy.

**Suppose one of you has a hundred sheep and loses one of them—what does he do? He leaves the other ninety-nine sheep in the pasture and goes looking for the one that got lost until he finds it. When he finds it, he is so happy that he puts it on his shoulders and carries it back home. (Luke 15:4-6*a*, TEV)**

> Too late have I loved you, O Beauty so ancient and so new, too late have I loved you! Behold, you were within me while I was outside: it was there I sought you, and rushed headlong upon these things of beauty which you have made. You were with me, but I was not with you. . . . You have called to me and have cried out, and have shattered my deafness . . . I have tasted you and I hunger and thirst after you. You have touched me, and I have burned for your peace.[12]

If we turn to God, we will find him as did the prodigal son. It will be: Welcome Home!

*Lord, it's such a comfort to my mind to know that I cannot drift beyond your love and care. It is a joy for me to think that your love is seeking me even when my self-centeredness is not seeking you. I thank you that you care that much. Help me to respond to your love. Amen.*

# 5
# LOVE

Was there ever a better sounding word than that? "I love you." Three little words we never grow tired of hearing. "Your love has lifted me higher and higher." "Love makes the world go round." Love songs. Love letters. Love poetry. Pictures of love. Thoughts of love. Expressions of love. But what is love? Is it a feeling and nothing more? Is it here today and gone tomorrow? Is it selfish and self-seeking? So much that we call "love" is not love. But "God is love." Everyone needs love, God's love. Everyone needs love from another person. Are you ready to receive love? Are you ready to give love? God's best to us is love—his love.

## Friends

We don't go far in life before we realize how important it is to have good friends. Unfortunately, as life moves toward its mid-stream and beyond, we find that if we have one or two people who accept us for better and for worse, we're truly blessed. I say "unfortunately" because it seems that we should develop more good friendships than that, but somehow most of us don't.

I don't know why we don't. Maybe it's a lack of time that makes us unable to cultivate friendships. Maybe self-centeredness prevents us. Perhaps we're too interested in what's happening to us and not interested enough in what's going on with others. Maybe it's because we lose confidence in people and thus find ourselves unable to trust our deeper selves to them. I really don't know why.

But I know we need friends. We especially need the kind of friends suggested by the old English word for *friend*—"free one." In the days of knighthood, a real friend had the freedom to enter the bedchamber of his friend. He was welcome in any room of the house. He was trustworthy. Nothing was kept secret from him, for the person could be assured that no judgment would be passed and no confidence betrayed. That type of person is hard to find.

Being "friendly" and being a "friend" are not synonymous with each other. A pleasant smile, a ready handshake, and a warm greeting are relatively easy to give. They're good gestures of kindness, but they're inexpensive. We can give these expressions of greeting to anyone without having to make a commitment of ourselves.

Being a "friend," however, can be costly. Friends have been known to make great sacrifices for one another. They have taken big risks. Sometimes they find it necessary to defend one another when the other is not around. They support each other emotionally and are available to each other in difficult times as well as the pleasant periods of life. Friends weep with each other. They rejoice with each other. They do all of this because of the nature of their friendship. They really care for one another.

One day Jesus said to Judas, "Friend, why are you here?" (Matt. 26:50, RSV). Judas had led the soldiers to the garden to arrest Jesus. Perhaps Jesus used the word *friend* to remind Judas of his treacherous act. It was as if he were saying to him—"Look, I opened my heart to you. I told you everything about myself. Now you have betrayed my confidence in you. You have delivered me to the enemy." Essentially, that's what it means to be a "traitor," to betray a friendship.

True friendship is based on love—the kind of love that is dependable. Maybe that's why we have so few truly good friends. Maybe it has something to say about our love. Maybe.

**After that, Saul's son Jonathan was deeply attracted to David and came to love him as much as he loved himself . . . Jonathan swore eternal friendship with David because of his deep affection for him. (1 Sam. 18:1, 3, TEV)**

> "A friend is one soul in two bodies." Yet friendship implies few friends rather than many; he who has many friends has no "friend"; and "to be a friend to many people in the way of perfect friendship is impossible." Fine friendship requires duration rather than fitful intensity.[1]

*Lord, thank you for being a Friend. Thank you for baring your self to me, for giving your love to me. As you trusted me, help me to learn to trust others. And, Father, help me to be your true friend as I would have others to be mine. Help me to be a true friend. In Jesus' name, I pray. Amen.*

## Together

Saint Exupery wrote, "Love does not consist in gazing at each other, but in looking together in the same direction." Do we really understand that statement? If we don't, it is extremely important that we learn what it means, because until we do we're going to experience an immense amount of disappointment and failure in some very important relationships.

"Love does not consist in gazing at each other." That's what many of us do, and that's all we do. We look at each other, expecting the other to fulfill all our needs and empty places. In a sense, it's a classic example of selfishness.

Let me illustrate. When two people who are married to each other look to each other for all their deep emotional fulfillment, they will be surprised to find the limitations of the other. It doesn't take long for a person to get "drained." When that happens, that one can no longer be a great source of strength. What happens then? Any number of things—resentment, bitterness, hostility, rejection, and maybe even divorce. "He no longer meets my needs," said one woman.

Even in the world of athletics, whenever people "gaze" at a team, admire a team, worship a team, and expect the team to meet all their needs for victory and success, they run the risk of great disappointment and frustration. So long as the team is winning, everyone is all right, but when the team loses, the shattered individuals build up great resentment, loss of faith, and even rejection of the athletes and coaches.

Sadly enough, the same is true about our relationship with God. If we come to God only for selfish reasons, then whenever God fails to "come through," when our prayers are not answered the way we prayed them, we have a tendency to lose confidence in him. We doubt his love. We might even doubt his existence.

What is the alternative to this? "Love . . . [is] in looking together in the same direction." For a couple in a relationship of marriage, business, or something else, it means "we-ness" instead of "me-ness." It means, "I'm with you. We're looking out at life together, side by side. Your success is my success. Your failure is my failure. We will win together. We will lose together. Our love will be strengthened as we walk together in the same direction."

The same could be said about the sport's fan and his favorite athletic team. We're looking at our opponents, together. We'll find our fulfillment as we struggle together side by side. You will play the game, and I'll encourage you. If we win, we win. If we lose, we lose. We're together.

And it's the same in our relationship with God. God and I will look at life together. We'll gaze at the problems, side by side. We need each other, but we must not run the risk of "draining" each other.

Maybe that's what Jesus really meant when he said, "Take my yoke upon you . . ." He was saying, "Let's walk, and work, and hope, and live together, side by side. Somehow when people learn to do that, they receive strength and encouragement from each other and their love grows deeper as life is shared. Remember—we're in this TOGETHER.

**Under his control all the different parts of the body fit together, and the whole body is held together by every joint with which it is provided. So when each separate part works as it should, the whole body grows and builds itself up through love. (Eph. 4:16, TEV)**

> Every human being has a great, yet often unknown, gift to care, to be compassionate, to become present to the other, to listen, to hear and to receive. If that gift would be set free and made available, miracles could take place.[2]

*Lord, it's so easy to depend too much on another person to meet all our needs. We have a tendency to want you and others to "make" us happy. Help us to recognize the need of looking outward in the same direction—together. Maybe then we'll learn what it really means to grow in our relationship with each other. Amen.*

## "He Ain't Heavy"

Several years ago there was a song that had a line which said, "He ain't heavy; he's my brother." It was the story of one lad carrying another, and it appeared to the observer as if the one being carried were too large to be carried. “He ain’t heavy,” said the one who was carrying the other, “he’s my brother.”

Carrying people might be one of the harder things we’re asked to do in life. When do we do that? We do it when somehow they can’t “carry” themselves—when they are unable to carry themselves—when some circumstance prevails that prevents them from carrying themselves. Life is filled with such situations.

Obviously, when one is sick, he needs to be “carried” by others. I’m not speaking of “carrying” in the context of actually “lifting” the other, although that certainly will be true in some instances. Rather, I’m speaking of a “caring” relationship in which the strength of one is employed to help the weaker one.

People who are sick very often need the comforting care of those who are well. They don’t need our criticism, impatience, judgment, or hostility. The burden of many sick people has been made lighter by caring people who “carry” them with their love, encouragement, understanding, comfort, and helpfulness.

If you carry your brother when he is sick, can you also carry him when he’s depressed and blue? Some can, and some can’t. Some people have the beautiful capacity to listen, to really hear the brokenheartedness of others. They enter into the disappointment and “feel” the pain of the person who has been stung by some loss or deprivation. Others feel frustrated and helpless. They listen and perhaps want to help, but they equate “curing” with “caring.” They want to be able to “cure” the despairing one. If they don’t know how to do that, it might be easy for them to withdraw from the hurting one. A loss of “care” is often felt by the one in pain. It’s difficult to “carry” someone who is downhearted and depressed. Sometimes it’s more difficult to carry that one than it is someone who is physically ill.

Have you ever wondered when your brother is the heaviest? It isn’t when he is sick or emotionally depressed. It’s when he has sinned. More specifically, it’s when his wrongdoing has hurt you. The sin weighs heavily on your mind. It might have a tendency to crush you beneath its weight.

General Oglethorpe once said to John Wesley, “I never forgive.”

And Wesley said to Oglethorpe, "Then, sir, I hope you never sin." Sinners ought to be more sympathetic with sinners, but so often we're not.

Forgiveness is difficult for us to give—especially the kind of forgiveness that holds no grudges, that has no strings attached. Of course, when we confess our sins to God, we like the idea that he not only forgives us but remembers our sins against us no more (see Hebrews 10:17). We don't easily do that.

I've seen light come into the eyes of the sick when they were comforted by tender hands. I've seen hope come into the eyes of the depressed when words of care were spoken to them. But I've seen tears of joy fall down soft cheeks when a sinner experienced forgiving love and acceptance from another person. It seemed as though God were there. I think he was!

**"Father," the son said, "I have sinned against God and against you. I am no longer fit to be called your son." But the father called to his servants. "Hurry!" he said, "Bring the best robe and put it on him. Put a ring on his finger and shoes on his feet. Then go and get the prize calf and kill it, and let us celebrate with a feast!" (Luke 15:21-34, TEV)**

Lord, never before today
Have I so deeply understood
The ugliness of my sin.
But never before today
Have I been so completely submerged
In the ocean of Your grace.[3]

*Lord, thank you for robes, and rings, and shoes, and celebrations. Thank you for the love and forgiveness those things represent. As you have so freely given these things to me, give me the strength to give love and forgiveness to others. Lord, help me to learn the art of "carrying" others the way you so often have had to "carry" me. Amen.*

## Happiness Is . . .

. . . Being able to say to that face in the mirror—"Hey, I really like you! You're a neat person."

. . . Being able to say to that person you married—"It's great being married to you. Thank you for sharing your life with me."

. . . Being able to talk with your parents or children about anything that is important to you and feeling no generation gap.

. . . Liking your place. Places are usually no better than we make them. Most places could be better than they are if we would accept them and work hard to improve them.

. . . Putting more than time into your work. One should never allow himself to dislike his work so much that his greatest pleasure is in leaving it. If your work is honorable, do it with pride.

. . . Loving your country—not as one might worship an idol—but as a gift from God to you. Be proud of your heritage.

. . . Creating friendships, not just responding to the attempts by others to be our friends.

. . . Being able to say, "I'm sorry," when you have offended, disappointed, or hurt another person. Being able to say, "I really do forgive you" when one who has offended, disappointed, or hurt you begs your pardon.

. . . Being able to accept the braces on your teeth, the glasses on your eyes, the hearing aid in your ear, the baldness on your head, the pacemaker on your heart, or the crutches on your leg.

. . . Overcoming prejudices against people of other colors, races, nations, religions, economic classes, political parties, and, in general, those who don't think as you think.

. . . Learning to share your privileges with the underprivileged, your food with the hungry, your clothing with the poor, your companionship with the lonely, your freedom with the imprisoned, your love with the unlovely.

. . . Being able to look back at yesterday and say, "Thanks, I needed that!"

. . . Being able to look forward to tomorrow and say, "I'm looking forward to that!"

... Being able to say to God, "I really love you. Thank you for all you've done for me. I'm looking forward to the future in your will."

... Happiness is all these things and more. It is the spirit in which we face life. It's a gift from God given to those who learn to live and love the way Christ lived and loved. It's a gift just waiting to be opened. It's a gift of love.

**Peace is what I leave with you; it is my own peace that I give you. I do not give it as the world does. Do not be worried and upset; do not be afraid (John 14:27, TEV)**

Lord, I laugh with delight
When I think of the common things
You use to prove Your Presence!
This noon, for example:
There I stood in the kitchen
Washing a head of lettuce
Pulling the leaves one by one
To get to the heart—
And suddenly, clear as a bell
I heard You say
*The closer you get to My heart*
*The more satisfying it is . . .*
And I was refreshed
But not from the lettuce.[4]

*Lord, so many people are unhappy. Is that the way you want us to be? I remember Jesus saying something about "rest" and "peace." Teach us how to find happiness. Help us to know that it's a by-product. Lord, help us to "lose" ourselves in serving you and others. Maybe then we'll find true happiness. In Jesus' name. Amen.*

## Loving Failures

In Lorraine Hansberry's play *A Raisin In The Sun,* the good mother cried out whenever others were condemning the ambitious boy who wanted the family fortune. She reminded them that we do not just love people when they do good. We need to love them also when they have failed. In fact, it's when they have failed that they need the most love and acceptance.

But that's hard for us to do, isn't it? People who have failed don't appear as lovely to us as do those who succeed. We might find ourselves "looking down" on them, perhaps even repulsed by their appearance. If we're not careful we can easily render deep emotional damage to the spirits of those who have disappointed us. Resentment and rejection are heavy burdens to carry.

Yet, "failures" need love, too. Failing to become what one desires to become has a severe effect on a person's sense of self-worth. When others voice displeasure or exemplify a hostile attitude, the person's misery is compounded.

People who fail are not as rare as we might think. Some people fail "big." That is, their failure is more widely known, more highly publicized, more pronounced. Political figures, renowned people, and those who occupy strategic positions of leadership often find their failings magnified according to their stature. Others fail, too. The so-called "little people"—those whose names we do not know—they fail. All of us sin and "fall short of the glory of God" (Rom. 3:23, RSV). We even fall short of our own expectations. Edward W. Hoch expressed it this way:

> There is so much good in the worst of us,
> And so much bad in the best of us,
> That it hardly behooves any of us
> To talk about the rest of us.

How does one learn to love "failures"? First, we must always be aware of our own weaknesses and failings. When we see others in trouble, we need to remember that it could be ourselves if not for God's grace. That kind of attitude makes us more tender and more tolerant of the failings of others.

Second, we must realize that people who fail are usually no more pleased with their failings than are we. People who are down don't need a foot on their chests; they need a hand to help lift them.

Third, we must learn to look beyond the failing and discover a person who needs love, forgiveness, and acceptance. Isn't that what Jesus did for the adulteress that day when it appeared as if there were going to be a public "stoning"? He didn't approve of her behavior any more than the rest of them, but he gave her a future with forgiveness and encouragement.

As a "failure" yourself, isn't that what you want? I do. Then let us practice the same. It might help another "failure" learn how to "succeed."

**If your brother sins, rebuke him, and if he repents, forgive him. If he sins against you seven times in one day, and each time he comes to you saying, 'I repent,' you must forgive him. (Luke 17:3*b*-4, TEV)**

> When, therefore, the gospel has invited men to forgiveness, it never has invited them to a light-hearted place where sins are condoned. It has called them to a cross. And they have always heard the cross saying to them that it was hard even for God to forgive. It cost. It cost just what it always costs when men forgive: love putting itself in our place.[5]

*Dear Lord, in a world filled with failures, of which I am one, let us not forget the One who succeeded in loving all people who fail. As I try to follow him, give me the ability and opportunity to rescue those who are perishing and lift up those who have fallen. Through Christ, our Lord. Amen.*

## Lord, I'm Confused

There are many people who see no rhyme or reason to their existence. Their circumstances, their problems, and their situations are such that it all seems hopeless to them. They look at the future—not with optimism and anticipation, but with dread and fear. Or perhaps they look at it with a certain kind of wistfulness that seems to say, "I'll be so glad when it comes and goes, and it's all over."

"Lord, I'm confused. I pray, but my prayers seem to go no higher than the ceiling and no farther than the reach of my voice. I search for meaning in my experiences, but I find very little."

What can one think about life? What can one think about the events that happen to us in life? First, we must understand that all things that happen are not good. Anyone who thinks that God is the author of every circumstance and every situation has assigned a guilt to him that he cannot and should not bear. All things are not good. All things are not the will of God.

Some of us might be going through the pain of a troubled marriage. Some might be having difficulties with children or parents. Some might have the fear of a disease either in one's own body or the body of someone very dear. Some may be having dreadful economic problems, and some might be trying to recover from the loss of a precious loved one. All things are not good. They're not good for us. They weren't good for Paul. They weren't good for Jesus Christ.

The Bible does not tell us that all things are good. It does say, however, that "God in all things works for good with those who love him, those whom he has called according to his purposes" (Rom 8:28, TEV). What does that mean?

First, it means that some good can be derived even from that which seems to be so bad. God can pick up the broken pieces of our lives and put us back together again. That's encouraging to me. It is consoling for me to know that no matter what has transpired in the past, God is able to use that for some good.

Second, for that good to become a reality, it will take work. Particularly does it take "God's work." All of us know that work takes time. It takes effort. And sometimes it takes cooperation. God can and will do the work, but he oftentimes needs our cooperation, our help. We must not sit back and expect him to do it all for us. He wants to work with us. Together we can make something good out of something that has been bad.

Third, it takes love. God works best with those "who love him." Love is self-giving. It reaches out. It trusts. Love submits itself. If our circumstances are to become better, we must love God and work with him to make them better.

Fourth, it takes submission. "In all things God works for good with . . . those whom he has called according to his purpose." That means we must be willing to let God work in and through us to bring his kingdom on earth as it is in heaven. That is his purpose.

Life can be better than it is. It can become much more than we ever thought possible. God can enter into our circumstances and give us a beautiful future. He loves us enough to want to do that. Do we love him enough to let him bring meaning out of our confusion? Do we?

**In view of all this, what can we say? If God is for us, who can be against us? . . . in all these things we have complete victory through him who loved us!" (Rom. 8:31,37, TEV)**

> "To you in this room who are seekers, to you, young and old who have toiled all the night and caught nothing, but who want to launch out into the deeps and let down your nets for a draught, I want to speak as simply, as tenderly, as clearly as I can. For God *can* be found. There *is* a last rock for your souls, a resting place of absolute peace and joy and power and radiance and security." . . . "Eternity is at our hearts, pressing upon your time-torn lives . . . calling us home unto Itself."[6]

*Lord, in the midst of so many messes, under the clouds of so much that is confusing, let me know the peace of your presence. Help me to love you enough to work with you to make my life and my world so much better than they are. Thank you, Father, for the promise of your love, your care, and your work. I'm ready to help. Amen.*

## New Life

In his book *Surprise Me, Jesus,* Herbert Brokering penned these thoughts:

Lord, I marvel at weather changes
A season goes and a new one comes to take its place.
It's like a relay race
that is never finished.
Life never quits getting new.[7]

Life really does never quit getting new. New days, new opportunities, new challenges, new threats to our security—just lots of new things. Some are good and some are not.

But most of us like new things. We like old things, too. We enjoy our old friends, old mementos of the past, old memories. But it's nice to get new things, to make new friends, to fashion new experiences that one day will provide us with more old memories.

The good news that God wants us to receive today is that life has newness as a part of it. Old things pass away, and all things become new (see 2 Cor. 5:17). Jesus talked to a man about the possibility of having a new birth. And that's exciting. Especially is it exciting when we look back and ponder what we have done with the old one. It's good to know that we have the possibility of new beginnings, new births, a change of season for the soul.

Each new day is somewhat like new life. No matter what a person did on yesterday, he can make a renewed commitment of his life and time on a new day. It's a fresh beginning.

Each new opportunity is like new life. All of us are more familiar with failure than we would like to be. We have drunk from its bitter cup. We have wept with broken hearts. We have felt the bottom, and perhaps we've wondered if we would ever be on top of things again. But God says, "Yes. Yes you can. Yes, you can go on. Rise, let us be going." We know we can't bring back the past and relive it. But we can learn from it. We can vow to make the present and future better for ourselves and others.

Each new challenge is like new life. We grow with our challenges. The weights challenge the muscles, and the muscles take the challenge. The weights won't change, but the muscles will. A new subject to be learned, a new crisis to be faced—these are challenges. When we accept the dare, when we face the challenge, when we give our best effort toward winning—we become stronger. And that's good.

But best of all, I'm thankful for the new life which one can experience through God's forgiving love. Nothing can separate us from that love. Nothing can cause him to love me less. And the wonderful thing about it all is that the best is yet to be.

> Life is so ever-present, an ever-living thing.
> Lord, you are the creator of all of it.
> Thanks for a world without end, Jesus.[8]

**Then the one who sits on the throne said, "And now I make all things new!" He also said to me, "Write this, because these words are true and can be trusted." And he said, "It is done! I am the first and the last, the beginning and the end." (Rev. 21:5-6*a*, TEV).**

> What is God's good time now? When will come our future and our hope? . . . The future comes today. It never comes as future. As future it is always coming and never arriving. It is always on the way but never the way we walk. The future comes as God's new today in accordance with its own yesterday, which is now our today. As such it comes as surely as the promises of God.[9]

*Lord, newness excites me. I love its bright, shining appearance. I love its freshness. I love the opportunities it brings. Thank you, Father, for new beginnings, and thank you, too, for beautiful endings. Amen.*

## Wrappings Without Gifts

The Christmas party was in full swing. Gifts were under the beautifully decorated tree, and excited youngsters were fumbling through them looking for their names. Candy and cookies, soft drinks, and hot chocolate had been prepared for the occasion. Everyone was so happy.

One child was there whom the other children often laughed at. They called him "the village idiot." It was true that he was mentally retarded, but he enjoyed being around children, laughing with them, playing with them, and laughing at their play. For him, the day was different.

As the names were called out and gifts were presented to the children, he watched and waited for his name. One by one the gifts were given. One child received a doll, another got a model car, and on and on it went. Finally, there was only one gift remaining. It was in a big box that was beautifully wrapped. The retarded boy's name was on the card.

Quickly he tore through the wrapping paper, throwing bits and pieces into the air. His eyes danced with glee, and saliva dripped from the corner of his mouth. It was a big moment. Ripping the cardboard from the top of the box, he looked for his gift. No, it couldn't be. It could never be. No one would do that! No one would be that cruel! But someone was that cruel. Someone had done that. Someone took the time to get a box, wrap it delicately with soft paper and tinsel, put a big bow on it, and tie a card with the retarded boy's name nicely printed on it. But inside the box, there was no toy, no gift. There was nothing. It was a cruel trick.

Sometimes life is like that. We're not retarded, but our names are printed on the boxes, the packages, the presents. We rip into them with the same excitement a three-year-old shows on a Christmas morning. But then, nothing! emptiness! And the box is not nearly as empty as is the pit in one's stomach, the words that won't form, the open space that is left in the mind.

Our problem is not like that boy's problem. We fail to realize that there are some things in life that can be nothing but "empty." They have always been empty. They have never satisfied the person's deepest needs. Oh yes, they look good on the outside. They're tempting. They promise us pleasure, a good time, and a lot of fun. But then, nothing! absolutely nothing!

There are millions of people who have spent a lot of time unwrapping their life's "presents." Sadly enough, they have discovered that all they had anticipated, all they had worked for, all they had lived for was not there. Their boxes contained no deep satisfaction, no fulfillment. Empty.

God has a gift he wants to give to each of us. His box is not empty. He wants to give his love to us—love in a person, a babe in a manger, a teacher on a dusty road, a healer in a marketplace, a Savior on a cross. He wants to give us his hope—hope in a person—hope that failure is not final, that death is not the end. God has a Gift which he wants to give. Receive it. You'll enjoy it through all eternity.

**For God loved the world so much that he gave his only Son, so that everyone who believes in him may not die but have eternal life. (John 3:16, TEV)**

> If each gift is a symbol of love, no matter how small the gift, then surely there must be a love, total and supreme, one that doesn't fail. This is what men intuitively await, and what they are seeking in the smallest gifts received each day. . . . The universal quest for gifts is nothing other than a seeking after God, by whatever name we may call him. For only the One who has made all things and who owns all things can give them without asking anything in return except our gratitude.[10]

*Lord, I have been deceived by life. Like that boy I have torn off the paper and ribbons only to find that what I was really wanting was not in the box. And then, I received your Gift. I timidly opened it, and you surprised me with the greatest joy I have ever known. Thank you for Jesus Christ. The life he has given me continues to give, and give, and give. Thank you. Amen.*

## A Face in the Straw

Those strangers had traveled long, and their journey had literally worn them out. It would have been nice had they been able to find a motel or hotel, just anything that had a bed. Overnight lodging would have done wonders for their tired bodies. But there was nothing—no bed, no shelter from the night's chill. It made no difference. The time had come, "and she brought forth her firstborn son, and wrapped him in swaddling clothes, and laid him in a manger" (Luke 2:7).

The sounds of the night were not the soft, whispering sounds one might hear at a nurse's station in a busy city hospital, nor were they the sounds of the occasional "ping" that pages a doctor or nurse to an uncomfortable patient. Instead, they were the sounds of the night, the sounds of animals munching their meal, the sounds of beasts stepping restlessly from one leg to the other on the crunchy straw.

The large, watery eyes of the cattle looked on as the virgin mother carefully and tenderly caressed the soft body of her baby. The braying of the donkey didn't seem to disturb the sleeping child.

His was a face in the straw, a face in a manger, but for the shepherds who left their flocks and went as the angels had directed them, it was a face in the sky, an eternally brilliant face, a face about which the angels sang a song of peace.

Just a face in the straw, a face in a manger, but for two old people, Simeon and Anna, it was a face that had more character and substance than any sermon they had ever been privileged to hear in their magnificent Temple. It was alive with meaning, pulsating with hope, promising salvation.

Our minds wander back over the years when a dove was dispatched from a rickety old ark in search of some promise of land. When it returned, it held in its beak a sprig of green taken from an olive branch. For Noah and that motley crew in the ark, it was a sprig of hope, a promise of land, a promise of tomorrow.

Once again, floating in a different kind of ark, lost and wandering humanity was floundering on the treacherous, unpredictable seas of an adventure called "life." Once again God sent out a Dove of peace, and humankind was asked to look toward an infant, a face in the straw.

It was God's little Son wrapped in warm blankets. Not much—just a baby! A face in the straw, but a face that was filled with hope, promising the future, carrying as it were in his tiny, clenched hand the green sprig of eternal life, and saying in words we cannot begin to comprehend, "I am the way, the truth, and the life" (John 14:6).

Just a face in the straw, just a stranger come to town, just a new teacher in the synagogue, just a man on a cross. With the gift of Christ God was saying to the world, "I love you."

**But when the right time finally came, God sent his own Son. He came as the son of a human mother and lived under the Jewish Law, to redeem those who were under the Law, so that we might become God's sons. (Gal. 4:4-5, TEV)**

The stable—my heart
The guiding star—Your perfect plan
The song—Just As I Am
The gift—my irrevocable Yes
The joy—Your immeasurable Love
The hope—The King Is Coming
Lord
This is my personal paraphrase
Of Christmas.[11]

*What more can we say, dear God? You have spoken. Your Word came to us wrapped in swaddling clothes, lying in a manger. We're spellbound. We can't respond adequately. We stand amazed in his presence. We thank you, Heavenly Father, for the way you chose to do it. We thank you every year for the privilege of celebrating your love in Christ's birth. We thank you. Amen.*

## So This Is Love?

Do you remember the first time you fell in love? I remember. I was in the second grade at the time, and the object of my affection was a little girl who wore her hair in pigtails. I knew I was in love when she presented me with a Valentine card on which she had written the words: "I like you. Do you like me?" Wow!

Someone said that love is that itchy feeling around the heart that can't be scratched. It's where we live, or don't live. It's what we have, or don't have. It either makes our world go around, or it stops it from spinning. The presence of love gives meaning and purpose to our existence. The absence of love gives depth to our darkness.

Songwriters and poets have expressed the virtues of love. Dramatists, novelists, and artists have given expression to their thoughts about love. But what is love? Is it the same to all of us? Are there different kinds of love?

So this is love? So what is love? There is a kind of love that is erotic in nature, a love that appeals basically to the senses, a love that makes us "feel" good. For some, that's all there is to love—eroticism. "I like you so long as you make me feel good." Maybe that's where love begins. Maybe it has to be that way.

Our attraction to one another is at the "sense" level. To see, to touch, to experience intimacy and closeness on the level of one or more of our five senses—that attracts us at first. And that's OK because we're physical beings. Feelings are important.

So this is love? So what is love? There's a kind of love that is "brotherly" or "sisterly" in nature. It's a love that shows human kindness and affection, a love that expresses itself in the sharing of life. A love relationship ought to include this kind of love, because life is meant to be shared. Burdens and joys are meant to be shared.

So this is love? So what is love? There's a kind of love that is deeper than feeling and greater than sharing. It's a love most of us know little, if anything, about. We haven't experienced it on the human level. "God is love."

Paul Scherer has reminded us not to think of love as if it told us what God is, but to allow God to tell us what love is. God has shown us what real love is.

Real love is self-giving. It's a love that has no strings attached, a costly kind of love, a love that even allows a Son to be crucified, a nonretaliatory love.

The world is a stranger to that kind of love. Marriages have a scarcity of that kind of love. Our institutions and relationships know little about that kind of love.

"To love is to commit oneself without guarantee." That's what God has done. One day his love looked down on a young man whose self-interest caused him to turn away from God's will. Then another day, somewhere, somehow it all changed. That young man, now an old man, took a pen and wrote: "The beginning of the gospel of Jesus Christ." We call it the "Gospel of Mark." God did not grind him into submission. His love won a tender victory. So this is love? So God is love. And the really good part is—God loves us. How's your love life?

**The greatest love a person can have for his friends is to give his life for them. And you are my friends. (John 15:13-14*a*, TEV)**

> Man cannot achieve love, generate love, wield love, as he does his powers of destruction and creation. When I love someone, it is not something that I have achieved, but something that is happening through me, something that is happening to me as well as to him. To use the old soap-opera cliché seriously, it is something bigger than both of us, infinitely bigger, because wherever love enters this world, God enters.[12]

*Our loving Heavenly Father, we thank you for your love. We thank you that you did not beat us into submission with an awesome wrath. You brought us to your side through the love of Jesus Christ. Lord, help us to learn how to love at your level. We need the other levels, too, but give us the joy of loving the way you have first loved. In Jesus' name, we pray. Amen.*

# 6

# Hope

Words may come and words may go. Some are harsh and dirty. Some are soft and syrupy. But "hope"? That's a healthy, hearty, robust word. It counsels us to "throw our shoulders back and hold our heads high." It shouts at us to "look, for there is a tomorrow." Life isn't over yet. God is alive. God is here. God is now. "Christ in you, the hope of glory" (Col. 1:27). "In thee, O Lord, do I hope." "Where there's life, there's hope." Nice words are hard to find. But *hope* is a nice word. Many are living with hope . . . hope that the future will be brighter than the present . . . hope that a cure will be found. As long as there is still hope, there will also be prayer. And God will be holding you in his hands. And that's God's best to you!

## Beginning Again

The process of redirecting our lives is often slow, painful, and very confusing. And yet it is a process many people face day after day.

For some people, it is the adjustment to a death. We don't easily overcome our grief. After the shock and the customary ways we have of burying our dead, we must then deal with life. We must learn how to handle situations without familiar faces, familiar voices, and familiar figures. Slow, painful, confusing—indeed it is!

For some people, it is the adjustment to a broken home. Divorce is one way of ending a marriage relationship. In some cases, it may be the only way. It's certainly not God's intention that love die and homes be broken. Yet, that does happen.

For some people, it is the adjustment to a new place. We're a mobile society. The thousands of moving vans on the highways each week remind us that people are on the move. New friendships must be made, new identities established, and we must grow accustomed to new places. All of this can be slow, painful, and confusing.

There are other adjustments that must be made. Someone becomes a marriage partner for the first time. Someone becomes a parent or grandparent. Someone graduates from high school and leaves home to go to college, into some career, or into the armed services. Someone's health changes, or there is a change in the health of some loved one. And all of this can be slow, painful, and confusing.

There is no easy way of getting around the tough situations. It isn't like taking an aspirin tablet to get rid of a headache. Not everyone will handle the situation exactly alike. It can be as slow as time, as painful as an injury, as confusing as a complicated laboratory experiment.

People want to help, and sometimes they do help. A trusted friend who will give comfort, care, and counsel can be worth his or her weight in gold. But when the words and presence of our friends are heard and seen no more, we must deal with our pain, our decisions, and our dilemmas in the quietness of our souls. We can be terribly lonely.

That's where God meets us—in the slow, painful, confusing process of beginning again. He promises us, "I will never leave thee, nor forsake thee" (Heb. 13:5). He reminds us that "as thy days, so shall thy strength be" (Deut. 33:25). He encourages us, "Come unto me, all ye that labour and are heavy laden, and I will give you rest" (Matt. 11:28).

And the truth of the matter is—he does. Today, whatever redirection your life must take, surrender yourself and your situation to him. His grace is sufficient.

> **I waited patiently for the Lord's help;**
> **then he listened to me and heard my cry.**
> **He pulled me out of a dangerous pit,**
> **out of the deadly quicksand.**
> **He set me safely on a rock**
> **and made me secure.**
> **He taught me to sing a new song,**
> **a song of praise to our God. (Ps. 40:1-3*a*, TEV)**

> We must never be tied to the past or spend our lives bewailing the years that are gone forever. . . . We may allow ourselves a glance back now and again, but don't live in the past. . . . Our God is living and active. He calls us onwards in courage and hope. Press on![1]

*Lord, I know you are a God who makes all things new. Help me as I face the newness of my present situation. Give me the ability to profit from my past but not be held prisoner by it. Give me the excitement to pursue my present and future with the hope that you are with me, always. Amen.*

## "The Wounded Cry Out . . . "

The city is a fascinating place with its endless rows of houses and apartments, its shopping centers and offices, its buses, sidewalks, and streets. I've watched the city grow. I've seen a horse farm become a busy shopping mall. I've seen farm land give way to subdivisions. I've seen people move into the city by the thousands, and the city has grown.

Yet there is something else going on in the city. Behind the scenes—within the walls of those houses and apartments, in the silence of the bedrooms—"the wounded and dying cry out" (Job 24:12, TEV). Those words were spoken by Job a long time before our population explosion. He added some other words to go along with them—"but God ignores their prayers."

I think it would be difficult to say the former without saying the latter, too. "The wounded and dying cry out, but God ignores their prayers." That's not a true statement about God, but it is a true statement about the way we sometimes feel about God.

Whenever a person is in the "pits"—whenever an individual is laboring in the dark night of the soul; whenever one has been pierced or stabbed by the sharp arrows of life—one sometimes feels as if God is absent, too. One may even have resentment toward God for allowing the pain and heartache to come.

In the narrative where Jesus met Mary and Martha after their brother had died, we hear the heart cry of one of the women, "Lord, . . . if you had been here, my brother would not have died!" (John 11:32). "If you had been here . . ." That's another way of saying, "God, if you wanted to do so, you could have prevented my pain." It's another way of saying, "but God ignores [my] prayers."

In the city, in the country, in the tiny village hamlet, anywhere people are gathered, "the wounded and dying [will] cry out," and someone will say, "but God ignores their prayers."

Sometimes it's the pain that comes from our great disappointments, our foiled plans, our losses, that causes us to wonder where God is. Sometimes it's the pain that comes from the words of a trusted friend, or that which emanates from our weaknesses and failures, and maybe that which comes from no other source than God. And in our despair we cry aloud, "God doesn't know I exist, and if he does, he doesn't seem to care."

To the woman who said, "If you had been here, Lord, my brother would not have died," Jesus said, "Your brother will rise to life" (John 11:21-23). We're also told in that same narrative that "Jesus wept." Those two responses are God's gifts to the wounded and dying. The first is the gift of the ultimate—eternal life, life which will know no sadness, no tears, no death. But until that time, God gives his compassionate, caring presence. "Jesus wept" (John 11:35).

We have a God who hears our prayers and answers our prayers. The answers will not always meet with our approval, but God knows best, and he loves best. The "wounded and dying" are always going to "cry out," but there is a God who says, "Trust me. I'll take care of you in life or in death."

**But after you have suffered for a little while, the God of all grace, who calls you to share his eternal glory in union with Christ, will himself perfect you and give you firmness, strength, and a sure foundation (1 Pet. 5:10, TEV).**

> Faith knows itself to be weak and uncertain, and yet like a reed it will survive the storm better than the proud oak. It knows that in this world it can never penetrate all the unfathomable mysteries of God, and yet, however tiny the light it receives from him, this is the only light that can really show it the way. Faith alone brings true peace.[2]

*Father, I confess to you that there are times when I doubt your love and mercy. When my burden is so heavy and my needs so great, when I pray so earnestly for your power to bless me and those I love, and when nothing seems to happen, I doubt. Lord, help me to have a trusting spirit even in the midst of my sadness and pain. I know you're there, and I know you care. Amen.*

## Missing the Fun

In an art museum, a man turned to the old curator who knew and loved each piece on exhibit and said to him, "I don't see anything to get excited about." To which the art lover responded, "Yes, but don't you wish you could?"

There's a great message that is contained in that little bit of dialogue. It reminds me of the many people who are alive but who are missing the real joy of being alive. Life has no color to them; it's all black and white. They themselves are a "drag" to be around. That is, they drag down the spirits of others with their negativism and sense of hopelessness. Complaining constantly, they look at everyone and everything and find something to criticize. To them, "Life is a rat race in which the biggest rats get the cheese." How dreadful it must be to think that way!

It also reminds me of those who have not opened their minds to receive the truly beautiful and lasting values of life. Some of us live life so close to the surface, so close to the bare necessities, that we fail to allow ourselves to think deeper thoughts or learn new things to appreciate. For one to really love art, he must study it. He must try to understand the mood and meaning of the artist. For one to really enjoy great music, he must listen to it with the ears of his imagination. He must see the tumbling waterfall or rippling stream which the composer saw. But most of us never look beneath the surface of things. Thus we miss much of the fun.

Elizabeth Barrett Browning spoke of the same thing in this way:

> Earth's crammed with heaven,
> And every common bush afire with God;
> But only he who sees, takes off his shoes—
> The rest sit round it and pluck blackberries.[3]

Plucking blackberries might be fun for those of us who enjoy eating them, but when you have a choice of eating blackberries or watching burning bushes that are "not consumed," it comes in a poor second.

The world is alive with the wonders of God not only in nature but in human nature, too. Some look and say, "I don't see anything to get excited about." And to them we say, "Yes, but don't you wish you could? You're missing so much!"

I like people who have learned to look for God in life. I enjoy people who see God's handiwork in a sunset or a mountain crested with snow. I like people who see God in the wrinkled smile of an aged saint or in the soft skin of a young infant.

How blest are those people who are able to see beyond the surface of things. How blest indeed are those who see life, who see others, who see splendid opportunities, who see God—and who can get excited about it all. There's joy in abundance for those who go far enough for the fun. I'd hate to miss it. Wouldn't you?

**You have a saying, "Four more months and then the harvest." But I tell you, take a good look at the fields; the crops are now ripe and ready to be harvested! (John 4:35, TEV)**

> Life can be very exhilarating when you set the affections and lay hold on something that holds you. It doesn't mean you will be happy all the time. Nobody is happy all the time. "Life," said Woodrow Wilson, "isn't all running to a fire. Not everything is exciting." But if we have the consciousness that what we do, however unnoticed, adds up to something with a bit of eternal significance, that it contributes some modest part to some great total God is adding up, life will take on an unexpected luster of glory, zest and meaning.[4]

*Lord, I thank you that you have placed so much beauty, so much wonder, so much excitement in so much of life. Forgive me when I concentrate on that which is negative to me and thus miss the fun of living. Give me your insight so that I may see the beauty and blessings of life. Help me to go far enough for the fun. Through Jesus Christ, I pray. Amen.*

## Memories

When I was a teenager and listening to the popular songs much the way my teenagers listen to them now, I remember a song that was my favorite. Everyone had to stop talking when that song was being sung. It spoke about New Year's Eve, doing the town, tearing goal posts down. It was a song about moments that we remember.

Nostalgia! That's what it was then. That's what it is now. The song was talking about memories—good, pleasant, exciting memories of ball games, parties, quiet walks, noisy fun, and all the rest. But now when I remember the song, I don't think so much about what the song described as I do about the song itself. For the song reminds me of a place, a time in my past, a day gone by. Do you do things like that? Don't you have songs that remind you of other times in your life, other places, other people?

Memories! They're good for us if we sniff them like we might smell the roses. They're not good if we try to swallow them as one might try to eat the flowers. We should draw everything we can from yesterday, everything that is lovely and good, everything that makes us glad we had the experiences. We should take a deep breath as we remember them, but we must not eat the daisies. Memories are to be seen and smelled, but not eaten.

Life, like "old man river," just keeps rolling along. From sunrise to sunset, from the swiftly passing seasons and years, from one experience to another until the end of time, it keeps moving.

Is that so sad? It shouldn't be. We like newness in other areas, don't we? We like new houses and cars, new clothes and games. Why not anticipate new days, new years, the future?

Perhaps one of the reasons why we don't look forward to new days and new years is because we have failed to see that God is a God who makes "all things new" (2 Cor. 5:17). The living God does not linger in the dead past as we sometimes do. "Our God is marching on." There are new mountains to be climbed, new seas to be crossed, new songs to be written and sung, new paintings to be painted, new books to be written, new lives to be touched. New! Always something new, just as each minute is new, each day is new, each year is new.

Paul could say, "The past? Some of it I love, some of it, I hate. There are places of which I am proud. There are places where I am ashamed. But it's all there—the hate, the love, the pride, the shame. I can't undo it. It's a part of history now. It's part of me. But this one thing I can do. This one thing I will do. I'll press on toward the prize" (Phil. 3:13-14, author's paraphrase).

As the days and years come and go, as time marches relentlessly on without pausing to catch its breath, some of us are following a God who is walking in front of us, preparing our way. We can triumphantly say, "Lead on, O King eternal." We have smelled yesterday's roses. We must now plant tomorrow's garden. It's good to look back, but we must not try to walk while facing back. As God leads, let us follow. Even now we're creating memories.

**When we were at Mount Sinai, the Lord our God said to us, "You have stayed long enough at this mountain. Break camp and move on." (Deut. 1:6-7*a*, TEV)**

> "I don't know Who—or what—put the question, I don't know when it was put. I don't even remember answering. But at some moment I did answer *Yes* to Someone—or Something—and from that hour I was certain that existence is meaningful and that, therefore, my life, in self-surrender, had a goal.
>
> From that moment I have known what it means "not to look back," and "to take no thought for the morrow."[5]

*Thank you, Lord, for moments to remember, beautiful, alive, exhilarating, refreshing. I confess that sometimes they cause me to wish for another day and to escape the responsibilities of this day. But I thank you for good memories. Lord, help me to live this day so completely and beautifully that one day I shall look back upon it as a moment to remember. Amen.*

## Is There Any Fun?

When Sir Wilfred Grenfell was doing medical mission work in Labrador, he had the occasion to share some of his experiences with a church. He told about the hardships that were encountered in the early days of the work. Afterward a lady offered her sympathy. "Oh, no," replied Grenfell, "you must have misunderstood me. I was having the time of my life."

Are you having the time of your life? Is there any fun in life for you? Is your work enjoyable? Not too many people are having the time of their lives. That includes our spiritual relationships and responses as well.

Some of us are not certain about what it means to "have the time of one's life." Some make that synonymous with pleasure, or leisure, or a life without responsibilities. "Eat, drink, and be merry" is the theme song of some people. For others, life would be more enjoyable if they had no obligations, no time schedules, no pressures.

Is there any fun in life? If there is, how far does one have to go to find it? Is there fun in marriage? If so, where does it begin? When does it start?

When does playing an instrument become fun? Is it in the early days of one's instruction when the music must be learned, the fingers disciplined to strike the right keys, and extreme concentration given to the playing of the simplest melody? Or is it when the person has gone far enough for the fun, when one has learned how to discipline one's mind, fingers, and feeling for the music? Watch a piano student who is just beginning to learn to play the instrument, and then watch someone like Liberace. Who is having the most fun?

Fun begins whenever a person gives his or her total self to an endeavor. Some players have fun playing baseball. Some politicians have fun working in government processes. Some mothers are having fun being mothers to their children. Some Christians are having fun following Jesus Christ.

What makes the difference? Perhaps the answer can be found in the word *love*. Love makes the difference. The love of the game, the love of the work, love for the children, love for God—the people who are having the most fun are ones who love what they're doing.

What makes the difference? Perhaps the answer can be found in the word *commitment*. Commitment makes a difference. Some people are committed to the game, committed to their work, committed to the children, committed to God. They're the ones who are having the most fun in life.

"So many [people] stand just outside," said Samuel Shoemaker. "You are half-way committed to Christ, and you have your reward in a heart which is half-happy." There is fun in life—for those who go far enough for the fun.

If you are serious about wanting to have fun being a Christian, commit all that you are and have to Jesus Christ. You'll find out what real joy is all about!

**Listen to the glad shouts of victory in the tents of God's people: "The Lord's mighty power has done it! His power has brought us victory—his mighty power in battle!" I will not die; instead, I will live and proclaim what the Lord has done. (Ps. 118:15-17, TEV)**

> The men to whom He held out the romance of religion were men who had paid the price of religion. And the price of romance in religion is the price of romance everywhere else—single-mindedness. You can't pursue a dozen ways of life at once; nor serve a dozen spiritual masters. There is fun in religion—heaps of it, quantities of it—for those who go far enough for fun.[6]

*Lord, when I remember the truly exhilarating times in my life, it seems that all of them bore the same characteristics—love and commitment. Help me to love you with all my heart, soul, mind and strength. Help me to love others as I love myself. And help me to make whatever commitment of my life that needs to be made in order to really have "fun" in living. In Christ's name, I pray, Amen.*

## What Do You Expect?

A few years ago on Lincoln's birthday a cartoon appeared in some papers. It was a picture of two men greeting one another and exchanging this dialogue. "Any news down in the village, Ezra?" "No, nuthin' at all. Jest a baby born down at Tom Lincoln's house. Nuthin' ever happens around here."

Nothing at all, just a baby named "Abraham" who was born at Tom Lincoln's house. Just an infant who someday would write the Emancipation Proclamation. Just a baby who would grow up to be one of the most beloved and respected presidents of all time. "Jest a baby born down at Tom Lincoln's."

Any news down in Bethlehem? "Naw, not much. Lot of people milling about. This crazy census the emperor wants might be good for business, but it sure isn't much for sensible living. Don't like all these strangers comin' to town. Too distractin'. Nowhere to walk even on the streets. Fact of the matter is, somebody said one poor woman had to have her baby in a stable. No room anywhere."

"Who was the woman? Did anybody say? Where was she from?" "I don't think anyone knows much about her or the kid. Heard somebody say she was one of those outsiders from Nazareth or someplace. If that be the case, the kid won't amount to much. Everybody knows that nuthin' good comes from old Nazareth."

Nothing! Nothing at all, except a baby named "Jesus," a little boy named "Jesus," a man named "Jesus." Nothing at all—except a teacher who "taught as one having authority." Nothing at all—except that "the Word was made flesh, and dwelt among us" (John 1:14).

It seems that for the most part the world has always been nearsighted. We have not been much for seeing oak trees in acorns or great leaders in infants, or a Savior in a manger. The world has never been much for expecting anything unusual, outstanding, or great.

"Expect nothing, and you'll never be disappointed," one person said. If "disappointment" is the only worry one has, perhaps that's good advice. God knows there's plenty in life to disappoint us. But that's not much of an outlook to have. It's too selfish for one thing. It's too pessimistic for another. It would make us very much at home with the villager, who said, "Nuthin'! Nuthin' at all. Nuthin' ever happens around here."

The birth of Jesus Christ is God's way of saying to the world, "Don't ever expect nuthin'." It's God's way of saying to all of us, "You don't understand my ways, so don't act as if you've got the last word." It's God's way of saying to humanity, "Look at what I'm doing. I'm starting at the bottom, the very bottom, down where hunger and poverty are, down where there is loneliness and rejection, and I'm picking the world up from the bottom. My hands are under the bottom piece, and I'm lifting it higher than it has ever been lifted before."

The birth of Jesus Christ is God's way of asking us to look at life with light in our eyes, to face the future with hope, to believe that with God all things are possible. It's God's way of saying, "I love you."

**The angel said to her, "Don't be afraid, Mary; God has been gracious to you. You will become pregnant and give birth to a son, and you will name him Jesus. He will be great and will be called the Son of the Most High God. The Lord God will make him a king." (Luke 1:30-32a, TEV)**

> Then about tomorrow: I know not what the future holds but I know who holds the future. This is the guaranteed basis for going ahead, face up, chin set, eyes forward like one entranced by a radiant, gleaming, though distant scene. The fact that He promises to go with us all the way should be accompaniment enough for total effort on our part. What better company does one need?[7]

*Lord, when I am tempted to believe there's no hope, no help, and no future, help me to remember that there was a time when you surprised us with a birth announcement. Amen.*

## The Caterpillar

I heard about two caterpillars who were inching their way along across the grass when they saw a butterfly pass overhead above them. They looked up and one nudged the other and said, "You couldn't get me up in one of those things for a million dollars." Little did he know that one day he would get up in "one of those things" and love every minute of it.

That might be a good parable about life. It tells us something about our limited vision, unawareness of our own nature, and inability to comprehend our own destiny.

Millions of people are crawling through life when God intended that we should fly. We have little, if any, real comprehension of the meaning of the words *abundant life*. Life, as we experience it, can be nothing more than dullness, routine, emptiness, and "crawling on our stomachs." Some say, "I'd like to experience more. I'd like to experience the joy of 'flying,' but I'm afraid I would fall." As one said, "I'd really like to be a Christian, but I don't think I could live up to it." That's not a new idea. It's the "caterpillar psychology" all over again—"You couldn't get me up in one of those things for a million dollars."

Admittedly there is a sense of helplessness and fear that one might have as he observes the height of the butterfly and perhaps even envies its ability. But what the caterpillar doesn't realize is that the butterfly is nothing more than a caterpillar who has undergone a life-changing transformation. Through the plan of God, the caterpillar has been equipped for a different level of life. In the butterfly's past, it too was a "crawler." That was BC—"Before Cocoon." Then a transformation took place—a death to one form of existence and a rebirth to another form. Now, flying is as natural as crawling once was.

That's the way God does things. Some of us once were

"crawlers." But that was BC—"Before Christ." Then a transformation took place—a death to one form of existence and a rebirth to another form. "When anyone is united to Christ, there is a new world; the old order has gone, and a new order has already begun." What God requires, he makes possible.

One can "crawl" until he or she dies. But how tragic that would be since God intended for us to "fly."

**But God's mercy is so abundant, and his love for us is so great, that while we were spiritually dead in our disobedience he brought us to life with Christ. It is by God's grace that you have been saved. (Eph. 2:4-5, TEV)**

> Indeed, living a spiritual life requires a change of heart, a conversion. Such a conversion may be marked by a sudden inner change, or it can take place through a long, quiet process of transformation. But it always involves an inner experience of oneness. We realize that we are in the center, and that from there all that is and all that takes place can be seen and understood as part of the mystery of God's life with us.[8]

*Father, is it possible that most of us have never realized the great plans you have for us? Is it possible that we spend most of our time "inching along on our stomachs" when you have meant for us to fly? Lord, let your power come into my spirit in such a way that I shall learn the joy of rising with Christ. In his name, I pray. Amen.*

## Just Beyond Reach

Herbert Brokering has captured in a poem some of the feelings many of us have about so many things:

> Lord, I had a song on the tip of my tongue,
> I could not sing it.
> It was on the tip of my finger;

I could not touch it.
It was on the top of my head;
I could not remember it.
It was at the bottom of my heart;
I could not find it.[9]

I wonder how many "songs" are just beyond our ability to sing, or feel, or remember. I wonder how many of them are buried deep within our hearts, but so deep that we cannot find them.

"I'm so close to being happy," the young woman said, "but not quite. My heart has too much pain for that." *If* is such a small word, but it is pregnant with so much meaning. It's a word that could change history, but all it does is remind us of the way history might have been.

There are victories just beyond our reach. We try hard to win our battles, to overcome our temptations, to conquer our moods. Many of these victories are close; they're on the tip of our fingers, but somehow we cannot touch them. How frustrating!

How can we learn to sing the songs, touch the music, remember the tunes, and sing them from our hearts? What would it take for most of us to be able to face life with a lively melody instead of a funeral dirge? What would it mean for me to move from defeat to victory? Is victory possible?

First, it doesn't start within me at all. It begins with a power that is beyond my own. It begins with God. God is the giver of the song. It is he who puts us in touch with ourselves and with life. He is the one who enables us to remember what it means to have a purposeful and meaningful existence.

Second, the song in the heart is written by the fingers of God on the tender, receptive mind of the person. "Tender," not hardened. "Receptive," not closed. One has to want the song of the soul. One has to be open to the work of God in his life.

Third, the song finds its best expression in the music it brings to the life of others. Some people have heard the orchestra long into the night after they have given their love and kindness to others.

I've got a feeling that the songs that "are just beyond our reach" could be sung by all of us if we were to get in touch with God, ourselves, and others. Have you a song you're not singing?

**I have complete confidence, O God! I will sing and praise you! Wake up, my soul! Wake up, my harp and lyre! I will wake up the sun. I will thank you, O Lord, among the nations. I will praise you among the peoples. Your constant love reaches above the heavens; your faithfulness touches the skies. (Ps. 108:1-4, TEV)**

Lord
You said so gently
So persistently
"Give Me your weariness
And I'll give you My rest."
I did—finally.
You did—immediately.
Then, Lord, I marveled
That I had waited so long.[10]

*Lord, I heard someone say, "Oh, the little more, and how much it is!/And the little less, and what worlds away!"* ("By the Fireside," Robert Browning). *Help me to move from the almost to the altogether. Help me to surrender my heart, my life, my all to you so that the song will be in my heart and mind, and then, Lord, help me to sing it. Amen.*

## Easter in Our Eyes

The soft breezes of the early morning were blowing gently through the meadow grasses. Hills usually windswept were virtually calm, and a heavy dew lay thick on the sod. All night long a woman had been unable to sleep. She tossed and turned on her bed. She cried bitter tears.

Grief is a heavy burden to bear. If you have known it, then you have known the agony of lying awake on the first night after the death while your mind worked overtime. So many thoughts of the past. So much to think about concerning the future. Life itself can take on a certain "past tense" feeling.

She went to the grave in Joseph's garden that Sunday morning while it was still dark. She might as well go; she couldn't sleep. We don't lose our attachment to a body even though we Christians believe that the spirit of the person goes on to be with God. We dress the body up for its interment. We surround it with fine silk and linen and place it in a stylish casket. We decorate its last earthly dwelling place with flowers. We do this because we must. Something within us impels us to do the best we can for the one who has passed from us.

So Mary, unable to sleep, unable to deal successfully with her oppressive grief, went to the garden very early on that Sunday morning.

It was a visit she would never forget, a visit she would talk about again and again, a visit others would talk about—even until now. She had gone there in search of Christ's body. She was found there by the Christ who had come to Bethlehem years before in search of people like her. She didn't recognize him at first. Why should she? Through eyes clouded with tears she thought she was looking at the gardener. "If you took him away, sir," she said, "tell me where you have put him, and I will go and get him" (John 20:15, TEV). The courage of the devout! Jesus was much bigger than she, much heavier than she, yet she felt as if there were nothing that could stop her love. She would carry him away and bury his body again.

Then it happened. He spoke her name. The accent was there. The tenderness was there. There could be no doubt. It was Jesus, Jesus alive, ALIVE! She grabbed him as if to say, "You'll never get away again. I'll never let you out of my sight." "No, Mary," he softly said, "go and tell the others."

Each year at Easter time, the lilies bloom just as they have bloomed so many years before. Each year the trees come alive with their buds and leaves just as they have done so many years before. Each year, at Easter time, we celebrate the Easter faith—the faith of the crucified and risen Lord, the faith that boldly proclaims, "Because he lives, I can face tomorrow."

With Easter in our eyes, we have the hope of our own resurrection and the resurrection of those whom we love. We also have the hope that our dreams and feelings can live because Christ lives. With Easter in our eyes, we always live in the light of God's eternal sunrise. There's always hope!

**Let us give thanks to the God and Father of our Lord Jesus Christ! Because of his great mercy he gave us new life by raising Jesus Christ from death. This fills us with a living hope (1 Pet. 1:3, TEV)**

> But the proclamation of Easter Day is that all is well . . . In the end, his will, not ours is done. Love is the victor. Death is not the end. The end is life. His life and our lives through him, in him. Existence has greater depths of beauty, mystery, and benediction than the wildest visionary has ever dared to dream. Christ our Lord has risen.[11]

*Thank you, Lord, for giving us hope, hope in life, hope in death. Thank you for meeting Mary in her hour of darkest grief. That taught me that I can count on you meeting me in those dark hours of my life. Thank you, Lord, for putting Easter in our eyes. Amen.*

## Leaving Yesterday

Sooner or later everyone has to leave some "yesterday" in his or her life. How does one do it? How does one get away from the past? How does one live in the present with so many memories of the past?

Those are heavy questions. There are no easy answers. But the questions deserve some type of an answer, because all of us have the questions in one form or another.

In the past there might have been a death, tragic or otherwise, that caused the music to leave your life and the light to leave your eyes. Deaths are not easy for us to adjust to. There are so many times in the present that reminds us of the past. Since we can't run away from our minds, changing locations will not solve all the problems. We must learn how to cope with the past.

In the past there might have been another type of death—the death of a romance, a marriage, a vocation, a dream. Pain overwhelms us when we think about it. Tears might fill our eyes. The feeling of failure can be a devastating and abysmal feeling. But the fact remains. The reality is all too real. What has happened has happened.

In the past there might have been some sin committed, even something that we have learned to call "radical" such as murder, adultery, robbery, or something that our society especially disdains. How does one face the future with the reality of moral failure haunting one's memory? We've got to find a way out of the wilderness because we have sin in our past.

When the people of Israel were counseled to leave Babylon and return to their home, the ancient prophet said, "Nor need you hurry forth, fleeing like fugitives, for the Eternal God goes in front of you and your rear guard is Israel's God" (Isa. 52:12, author's paraphrase). In that bit of advice there is a recipe for walking away from yesterday.

"Walk, don't run!" A fugitive runs, because he's afraid of being caught. We should not have the "fugitive mind" in us. Every experience has something to teach us. We can learn from our pain, our sorrow, even our sins. We must accept the reality that there has been a "captivity," a time of sorrow, a time of pain, a time of sin. We must learn all we can from it.

"Leave, don't stay!" We must not allow yesterday to hold us a prisoner as a spider might hold a fly in its web. Relish the victories from the past—remember them, but leave them and search for other victories. Regret the losses—remember them, too—but leave them in the hands of a loving and forgiving God who can heal our brokenness.

"Look for God!" "The Eternal God goes before you." God is in front of us, leading us, clearing a path for us, caring for us. As one said, "I arrive nowhere but that God has been there." Look for him! "Your rear guard is Israel's God." That's a good thought—

God walking ahead of me—God walking behind me. As God walks behind us, he has a way of "cleaning up yesterday's mess." He forgives our sins. He heals our broken spirits. He gently closes the doors to the rooms we have left. Isn't it nice to have a God like that?

**I do not claim that I have already succeeded or have already become perfect. I keep striving to win the prize for which Christ Jesus has already won me to himself. Of course, my brothers, I really do not think that I have already won it; the one thing I do, however, is to forget what is behind me and do my best to reach what is ahead. (Phil. 3:12-13, TEV)**

> Is it worthwhile to listen to [Jesus' Sermon on the Mount]? It does not say: you *must* begin a new life! As if we could do such a thing anyhow, as if we were even willing to *listen* to such a thing! What it says is: something has happened in the province of life and you must allow it to give its signal to you. And then because that signal has been given, you can start afresh; life can begin again.[12]

*Lord, that's what I want—a new beginning! I know that one can never get away from the past, and I really don't want to do that, but I'd like to be able to have a fresh approach to the rest of my journey in life. Father, if you'll walk behind me and straighten that part out, if you'll walk before me and give direction to my life, if you'll dwell within me giving me strength for the day, I think I can travel. Amen.*

# Now

Lord
I don't ask You to renovate me
Nor do I ask You to reconstruct me
Or make me over.
I don't even ask You to patch me up
Or pare out the bruised spots
Or gloss over the tin and tarnish.
Rather, dear Lord, I ask You
To make a new species—
Something that never before existed.
Impart to me Your very own Life.
After all, Lord
It is such a simple thing for You
To create something beautiful
From a shapeless, chaotic mass.
It is such a simple thing for You
To divide light from darkness.
Please do it for me—now.

*Child of My Infinite Plan*
*Two thousand years ago*
*All you have asked I did.*
*Please accept it from Me—now.*[13]

# Notes

## *Chapter 1*

1. William Shakespeare, *Macbeth,* V, v, 26-28.
2. Helmut Thielicke, *Life Can Begin Again* (Philadelphia: Fortress Press, 1963), p. 11.
3. Dr. Seuss, *Yertle the Turtle & Other Stories,* an adaptation (New York: Random House, 1950).
4. Cecil Osborne, *The Art of Understanding Yourself* (Grand Rapids: Zondervan Publishing House, 1968), p. 170.
5. Roy O. McClain, *If With All Your Heart* (Old Tappan: Fleming H. Revell, 1957), p. 132.
6. Dwight Carlson, *Run and Not Be Weary* (Old Tappan: Fleming H. Revell, 1974), pp. 113, 114.
7. Paul Tournier, *The Adventure of Living* (New York: Harper & Row, 1965), p. 140.
8. Harry Emerson Fosdick, *What Is Vital in Religion* (New York: Harper Brothers, 1955), p. 41.
9. J. Wallace Hamilton, *Who Goes There: What & Where Is God* (Old Tappan: Fleming H. Revell, 1958), p. 21.
10. J. Wallace Hamilton, *What About Tomorrow?* (Old Tappan, New Jersey: Fleming H. Revell Co., 1972), pp. 166-67.
11. Paul Tournier, *The Person Reborn* (New York: Harper & Row, 1966), p. 70. Used by permission.
12. D. Martyn Lloyd-Jones, *Studies in the Sermon on the Mount,* Vol. 2 (Grand Rapids: Wm. B. Eerdmans, 1960), p. 72.

## *Chapter 2*

1. Henri J. M. Nouwen, *Making All Things New: An Invitation to Life in the Spirit* (San Francisco: Harper & Row, 1981), p. 57. Used by permission.
2. John Killinger, *For God's Sake, Be Human* (Waco: Word Books, 1970), p. 139.
3. Carlson, *Run and Not Be Weary,* p. 196.
4. McClain, *If With All Your Heart,* p. 132.
5. Ruth Harms Calkin, *Lord, You Love to Say Yes* (Elgin, Illinois: David C.

Cook Publishing Company, 1976), p. 46. Used by permission.
6. Phillips, *For This Day,* p. 17. Used by permission.
7. Paul Tournier, *The Adventure of Living* (New York: Harper & Row, 1963), p. 192. Used by permission.
8. Shakespeare, *King Lear,* V, iii, 9-19.
9. McClain, *If With All Your Heart,* p. 122.
10. Robert K. Greenleaf, *Servant Leadership* (New York: Paulist-Newman Press, 1977), p. 16.
11. Ruth Harms Calkin, *Lord, You Love to Say Yes* (Elgin, Illinois: David C. Cook, 1976), p. 49.
12. Paul Tournier, *The Meaning of Persons* (Philadelphia: The Westminster Press, 1964), p. 158.

## *Chapter 3*

1. Henri J. M. Nouwen, *Making All Things New,* p. 36. Used by permission.
2. Henri J. M. Nouwen, *Out of Solitude* (Notre Dame: Ave Maria Press, 1974), p. 59.
3. Sören Kierkegaard, trans. by David Swenson, *Works of Love* (New York: Harper & Row, 1962), p. 39.
4. Paul Tournier, *Escape from Loneliness* (Philadelphia: The Westminster Press, 1962), p. 170. See acknowledgment on copyright page.
5. McClain, *If With All Your Heart,* p. 34.
6. William Barclay, *Turning to God* (Philadelphia: Westminster Press, 1964), pp. 40, 41.
7. Rollo May, *The Art of Counseling* (Nashville: Abingdon Press, 1939), p. 159.
8. Thomas a Kempis, *The Imitation of Christ* (London: Collins, 1957), pp. 148, 149.
9. Paul Tournier, *Learn to Grow Old* (New York: Harper & Row, 1972), p. 74. Used by permission.
10. John Killinger, *Bread for the Wilderness, Wine for the Journey* (Waco: Word Books, 1977), p. 11.
11. Elton Trueblood, *A Place to Stand* (New York: Harper & Row, 1969), p. 43. Used by permission.

## *Chapter 4*

1. Tournier, *Escape from Loneliness,* p. 115.
2. Ibid., p. 116.
3. Osborne, *The Art of Understanding Yourself,* p. 155.
4. Ruth Harms Calkin, *Tell Me Again, Lord, I Forget* (Elgin, Illinois: David C. Cook, 1974), p. 17. Used by permission.

5. Tournier, *Escape from Loneliness*, p. 115.

6. Paul Tillich, *The Shaking of the Foundations* (London: SCM Press, 1949), p. 182.

7. Sigmund Freud, *A General Introduction to Psychoanalysis* (New York: Washington Square Press, Inc.), p. 22.

8. John S. Whale, *Christian Doctrine* (Cambridge: The University Press, 1956), p. 146.

9. William Blake, "Auguries of Innocence."

10. Morris E. Eson, *Psychological Foundations of Education* (New York: Holt, Rinehart, and Winston, 1964), p. 39.

11. Francis Thompson, "The Hound of Heaven," *The World's Great Religious Poetry,* comp. by Caroline Miles Hill (New York: The Macmillan Company, 1938), p. 45.

12. Augustine, *The Confessions of Saint Augustine,* ed. John K. Ryan (Garden City: Doubleday, 1960), p. 254 f.

## *Chapter 5*

1. Will Durant, *The Story of Philosophy* (New York: Garden City Publishing Company, 1943), p. 62.

2. Henri J. M. Nouwen, *Out of Solitude* (Notre Dame: Ave Maria Press, 1974), pp. 40-41.

3. Ruth Harms Calkin, *Lord, I Keep Running Back to You* (Wheaton, Illinois: Tyndale House Publishers, 1979), p. 14. Used by permission.

4. Ruth Harms Calkin, *Tell Me Again, Lord, I Forget,* p. 63. Used by permission.

5. Harry Emerson Fosdick, *The Secret of Victorious Living* (New York: Harper & Row, 1934), p. 117.

6. Thomas R. Kelly, *A Testament of Devotion* (New York: Harper & Row, 1941), pp. 18, 29.

7. Reprinted from *Surprise Me, Jesus* by Herbert T. Brokering, copyright 1973, by permission of Augsburg Publishing House.

8. Ibid., p. 46. Used by permission.

9. Nels F. S. Ferré, *The Extreme Center* (Waco: Word Books, 1973), p. 26.

10. Paul Tournier, *The Meaning of Gifts* (Richmond, Virginia: John Knox Press, 1963), p. 58 f.

11. Calkin, *Tell Me Again, Lord, I Forget,* p. 52. Used by permission.

12. Frederich Buecher, *The Magnificent Defeat* (New York: The Seabury Press, 1966), p. 34.

## *Chapter 6*

1. Phillips, *For This Day,* p. 253.

2. Paul Tournier, *The Person Reborn* (New York: Harper & Row, 1966), p. 175. Used by permission.

3. Elizabeth Barrett Browning, "Aurora Leigh," *The Poetical Works of Elizabeth Barrett Browning* (New York: James Miller, 1872), p. 452.

4. J. Wallace Hamilton, *Serendipity* (Old Tappan, New Jersey: Fleming Revell, 1965), p. 61.

5. Dag Hammarskjold, *Markings* (New York: Alfred A. Knopf, 1964), p. 205.

6. Sam Shoemaker, *Extraordinary Living for Ordinary Men* (Grand Rapids: Zondervan Books, 1965), p. 17.

7. McClain, *If With All Your Heart*, p. 188.

8. Henri J. M. Nouwen, *Making All Things New* (San Francisco: Harper & Row, 1981), pp. 57-58.

9. Brokering, *Surprise Me, Jesus*, p. 14. Used by permission.

10. Ruth Harms Calkin, *Lord, I Keep Running Back to You*, p. 19. Used by permission.

11. Buechner, p. 81.

12. Thielicke, *Life Can Begin Again*, p. xv.

13. Calkin, *Lord, I Keep Running Back to You*, pp. 20, 21. Used by permission.